THE BORDERS ABBEYS WAY

THE ABBEYS OF MELROSE, DRYBURGH, KELSO AND JEDBURGH IN THE SCOTTISH BORDERS

by Paul Boobyer

JUNIPER HOUSE, MURLEY MOSS,
OXENHOLME ROAD, KENDAL, CUMBRIA LA9 7RL
www.cicerone.co.uk

© Paul Boobyer 2019
First edition 2019
ISBN: 978 1 85284 980 1

Printed in China on behalf of Latitude Press Ltd.
A catalogue record for this book is available from the British Library.
All photographs © Lorna Anness unless stated otherwise.

© Crown copyright 2019 OS PU100012932

Town mapping by Lovell Johns www.lovelljohns.com
© Crown copyright 2019 OS PU100012932. NASA relief data
courtesy of ESRI

For Lorna, with whom, by great fortune, I travel life's pathway.

Updates to this Guide

While every effort is made by our authors to ensure the accuracy of guide-books as they go to print, changes can occur during the lifetime of an edition. Any updates that we know of for this guide will be on the Cicerone website (www.cicerone.co.uk/980/updates), so please check before planning your trip. We also advise that you check information about such things as transport, accommodation and shops locally. Even rights of way can be altered over time. We are always grateful for information about any discrepancies between a guidebook and the facts on the ground, sent by email to updates@cicerone.co.uk or by post to Cicerone, Juniper House, Murley Moss, Oxenholme Road, Kendal, LA9 7RL.

Register your book: To sign up to receive free updates, special offers and GPX files where available, register your book at www.cicerone.co.uk.

Front cover: Melrose Abbey (Stage 1)

CONTENTS

Kelso Abbey (Stage 2)

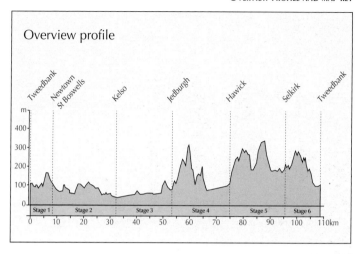

Overview profile

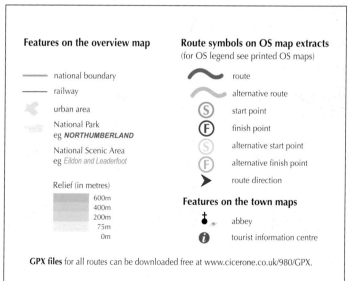

Features on the overview map

━━━ national boundary

━━━ railway

urban area

National Park
eg **NORTHUMBERLAND**

National Scenic Area
eg *Eildon and Leaderfoot*

Relief (in metres)

600m
400m
200m
75m
0m

Route symbols on OS map extracts
(for OS legend see printed OS maps)

〜 route

〜 alternative route

(S) start point

(F) finish point

(S) alternative start point

(F) alternative finish point

➤ route direction

Features on the town maps

♄ abbey

𝒊 tourist information centre

GPX files for all routes can be downloaded free at www.cicerone.co.uk/980/GPX.

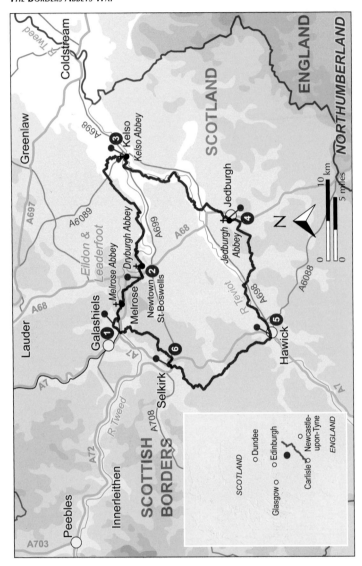

8

ROUTE SUMMARY TABLE

Stage	Start	Finish	Distance	Ascent	Time	Page
1	Tweedbank Railway Station NT 523 348	Langlands Place, Newtown St Boswells NT 576 318	4.8 miles (7.7km)	160m	2hr	32
1 (alt)	Tweedbank Railway Station NT 523 348	Dryburgh Abbey Hotel NT 590 318	6.1 miles (9.7km)	155m	2hr 20min	32
1 (alt)*	Tweedbank Railway Station NT 523 348	Clint Lodge (Clintmains) NT 604 327	8 miles (12.8km)	185m	3hr	32
1 (alt)*	Tweedbank Railway Station NT 523 348	Main Street, St Boswells NT 593 309	5.7 miles (9.2km)	198m	2hr 15min	32
2	Langlands Place, Newtown St Boswells NT 576 318	The Square, Kelso NT 727 339	15 miles (24.2km)	302m	5hr 30min	41
3	The Square, Kelso NT 727 339	Abbey Place, Jedburgh NT 650 205	13.5 miles (21.7km)	268m	5hr	51
4	Abbey Place, Jedburgh NT 650 205	Teviotdale Leisure Centre, Hawick NT 505 153	13.1 miles (21.1km)	547m	5hr 15min	61
5	Teviotdale Leisure Centre, Hawick NT 505 153	Market Place, Selkirk, NT 469 284	12.6 miles (20.3km)	583m	5hr 15min	70
6	Market Place, Selkirk, NT 469 284	Near Tweedbank Railway Station NT 529 347	8.9 miles (14.4km)	336m	3hr 35min	78

*St Boswells is 0.9 miles (1.5km) off the Borders Abbeys Way and Clint Lodge is 600 metres off the Borders Abbeys Way

The path follows a branch of the former Waverley Line near Jedburgh (Stage 3)

INTRODUCTION

Black Hill – an ancient volcano just north of Newtown St Boswells (Stage 1)

The Borders Abbeys Way links four of Britain's grandest ruined medieval abbeys in the enchanting landscape of the central Scottish Borders. The route is a well waymarked, 68-mile (109km) circuit and is one of Scotland's Great Trails. The variety of terrain and views along the Way will delight even the most seasoned walkers.

This guidebook provides a comprehensive description of the route, which passes through the towns of Melrose, Kelso, Jedburgh, Hawick and Selkirk and the villages of Denholm and Newton St Boswells. It also provides information on a variety of sites of historical and cultural interest (including the abbeys), accommodation available in each town en route,

and detailed bus service information to assist planning stages of the route as stand-alone day walks.

The abbeys and other historical sites encountered along the route tell the tale of a series of conflicts between the kingdoms of England and Scotland that took place between the mid 12th and early 17th centuries; a time when the Borders region was a dangerous and lawless frontier. The repeated vandalism and eventual destruction of the abbeys, the construction of fortified tower houses and the marauding militias known as *reivers*, were a product of this turbulent socio-political milieu. A walk on the Borders Abbeys Way will connect you with this fascinating period of history; indeed, some of the paths on the Way are the very same routes that monks and abbey staff used to travel between the Borders abbeys, and no doubt were also used by the notorious reivers.

THE BORDERS ABBEYS WAY

The Way comprises paths alongside the Tweed and Teviot rivers, forest tracks, historic drove roads and disused railway lines, and traverses farmland and open hills. Most of the route is off-road, although there are some stretches walking on quiet, minor roads. The gradients are mostly gentle, and the altitude is never more than 338 metres, yet the views are frequently impressive.

The route can be undertaken at any time of year and can be reached within an hour by rail from the centre of Edinburgh. By bus it is just over an hour from Berwick-upon-Tweed, an hour and a half from Carlisle, and three hours from Newcastle. Frequent local buses connect each town along the Way.

The circuit is described in a clockwise direction. Most people complete the route in six days:

- Tweedbank to Newtown St Boswells via Melrose 4.8 miles (7.7km)
- Newtown St Boswells to Kelso via Dryburgh 15 miles (24.2km)
- Kelso to Jedburgh 13.5 miles (21.7km)
- Jedburgh to Hawick 13.1 miles (21.1km)
- Hawick to Selkirk 12.6 miles (20.3km)
- Selkirk to Tweedbank 8.9 miles (14.4km)

The purple flowers of rosebay willowherb (Stage 4)

OTHER LONG-DISTANCE WALKS CONNECTING WITH THE BORDERS ABBEYS WAY

- Southern Upland Way connects with a portion of Stage 1
- St Cuthbert's Way connects with portions of Stages 2 and 3
- Cross Borders Drove Road connects at Hawick (Stage 4 end/Stage 5 start)

Alternative endings to Stage 1 are Dryburgh Abbey Hotel, which would extend Stage 1 by 1.3 miles (2km), and a B&B at Clintmains, which would extend Stage 1 by 3.2 miles (5km). Stage 2 would thus be respectively reduced to 13.7 miles (21.9km), or 11.8 miles (18.9km). Another alternative ending is St Boswells, 0.9 miles (1.5km) off the Borders Abbeys Way, just east of Newtown St Boswells.

The Borders Abbeys Way is suitable for people with a moderate level of fitness. The choice of accommodation, restaurants, cafés and other facilities on the route will appeal to people who enjoy staying in comfortable accommodation, eating quality cuisine and visiting sites of historical interest, museums and country estates. Luggage transfer services are available from Walking Support (see Appendix D for contact information).

An entrance fee is charged at Melrose, Dryburgh and Jedburgh abbeys, where there are interpretation centres and gift shops. There are also museums at Melrose and Jedburgh abbeys. Entrance to the ruins of Kelso Abbey is free of charge. The ruins of all the abbeys are managed by Historic Environment Scotland (HES). An Explorer Pass provides access to Melrose, Dryburgh and Jedburgh abbeys, as well as to the impressive Smailholm Tower, a fortified tower house built by a local reiving family; and the sinister, semi-ruined Anglo-Norman Hermitage Castle. The Explorer Pass can be purchased from HES via their website (see Appendix D), from the venues listed above, or any Visit Scotland visitor information centre. If five or more HES properties are accessed with this pass, entry is at a discounted rate.

ALL ABBEY OPENING TIMES

Apr–Sept daily 9.30am–5.30pm
Oct–Mar daily 10am–4pm
(Kelso Abbey closed Thu–Fri Oct–Mar)

HISTORY OF THE BORDERS ABBEYS

The four magnificent ruined abbeys at Melrose, Dryburgh, Kelso and Jedburgh are testament to the power and wealth of medieval Anglo-Norman monasticism. Founded in the first half of the 12th century at the behest of King David I of Scotland (1084–1153) by monks and canons whose religious orders originated in Normandy, the abbeys were key to David's Normanisation of Scottish society and to the introduction of the feudal system to Scotland – reforms which have been termed the 'Davidian Revolution' by some historians. These reforms empowered the Roman Catholic Church, which administrated the infrastructures of taxation, land management and international trade on behalf of the monarchy.

The monks and canons were skilled agriculturalists and merchants and applied new farming techniques to the extensive abbeys' estates, which included some of the best arable land in Scotland. The abbeys also controlled the lucrative wool trade, exporting to the major trading ports of northern Europe, generating huge revenues. In addition, they were the locus of education, and noble families often sent their sons to be schooled by the monks. Kelso Abbey, in particular, had a renowned library in the Medieval Period.

King David, whose first language was French, was the first Anglo-Norman king to sit on the Scottish throne – his father, Malcolm III of Scotland (1031–1093), and the kings that preceded him, had spoken Gaelic. From a young age David had been groomed to be an Anglo-Norman ally by King Henry I of England (1068–1135) and had spent most of his teenage years and early adulthood at the (Norman, French-speaking) English royal court and in Normandy prior to his ascension to the Crown of Scotland – to which he had only a tenuous claim. After his coronation, backed by King Henry (a son of William the Conqueror (1028–1087)), David married Henry's sister, effectively unifying the kingdoms of England and Scotland.

However, after the death of King Henry in 1135, the two kingdoms fought for supremacy. Hostility was intensified by rivalry within the Church that led to the separation of the Scottish Church from its English base. The Borderlands consequentially became a stark frontier between the warring kingdoms, and for the following four centuries the abbeys and inhabitants of the Borderlands suffered the lawlessness and frequent waves of violence that swept the region.

The abbeys were attacked by English armies on several occasions and were subsequently rebuilt or repaired. But the ruins we see today are the result of campaigns led by the Earl of Hertford in 1544 and 1545. The Earl, acting on behalf of the Protestant King Henry VIII of England (1491–1547), intended to end Catholic hegemony in Scotland. This was finally achieved in 1560 with the Scottish Reformation, although the hapless monks and canons incumbent in the abbeys during the Reformation were permitted to continue living in the ruins.

Melrose Abbey

Founded in 1136 by monks of the Cistercian Order, Melrose Abbey is considered to be one of the most beautiful ruined abbeys in the United Kingdom.

King David had wanted the abbey to be sited two miles to the east, on the ruins of an earlier Celtic monastery founded by Saint Aidan in AD635, but the monks persuaded the king to accept the current site, claiming it was more suitable for agriculture. In addition, the new site was on the main route connecting Edinburgh to England, which had the advantage of being a paved Roman road (Dere Street), and was ideally situated to provide accommodation, food and other services to travellers.

A carving on Melrose Abbey. Many of these were destroyed in 1544 by the English (Stage 1)

In 1322 most of the abbey was destroyed by the army of King Edward II of England (1284–1327) and was burned down again 63 years later by King Richard II of England (1367–1400), causing such severe damage that masons took more than a century to rebuild the abbey.

It is claimed that Melrose Abbey contains the heart of Robert the Bruce, King of Scots (1274–1329), whose organ was allegedly buried there in 1330 or 1331 (the rest of his body was interred at Dunfermline Abbey). In 1996 a lead container, which may contain the King's heart, was found buried below the abbey's chapter house floor. The container was never opened and was reburied at the abbey on 22 June 1998. King Alexander II of Scotland (1198–1249) is also buried at the abbey.

King David's step-brother, Waltheof, was the second abbot of Melrose Abbey from 1148 until his death in 1159.

Melrose Abbey was severely damaged during a bombardment led by the Earl of Hertford in 1544, and was never rebuilt. If you look carefully around Melrose, you will see pieces of carved masonry from the abbey incorporated into buildings and walls.

Dryburgh Abbey

Dryburgh Abbey, built in 1150 by canons of the Premonstratensian Order, is situated on the banks of the River Tweed about four miles east of

The grand ruin of Melrose Abbey (Stage 1)

Melrose. The site has a long history of religious continuity, and historical documents indicate that the abbey was constructed on the remains of an earlier Celtic monastery.

The medieval abbey was founded with the agreement of King David by Hugh de Morville, an Anglo-Norman noble and High Lord Constable of Scotland. However, the abbey struggled financially over the years, in part due to its lack of royal patronage.

In 1316 King Robert the Bruce (1274–1329) used Dryburgh Abbey as a base for raiding forays into England. Campaigns of retribution by the English King Edward II in 1322 led to the abbey being looted and severely damaged by fire. Dryburgh and the other Borders abbeys remained as possessions of King Edward until the middle

of the 14th century, at which point the region reverted to control of the Scots, now ruled by King David II of Scotland (1324–1371). Enraged by his losses, King Edward mounted a ferocious campaign of retribution which led to Edinburgh being sacked and burned. Returning to England through the Borders region, Edward's armies again looted and set fire to Dryburgh Abbey. The abbey was destroyed by fire for a third time in 1443, although this time allegedly by accident.

Despite having been set on fire three times, the chapter house features paintwork that dates back to its construction. Both the chapter house and the cloister are very well preserved and are some of the finest examples of Gothic church architecture in Scotland.

Sir Walter Scott, one of Scotland's best-known writers, is buried at the abbey. Sir Walter, who resided at Abbotsford House at Tweedbank (on Stage 6 of the Borders Abbeys Way), had a huge fondness for the Borders region, and some of his work includes stories based on Borders ballads and folklore. Field Marshall Sir Douglas Haig, commander of British forces on the Western Front from 1915 until the end of World War I, is also buried within the abbey grounds. Haig, who presided over the Battle of the Somme, is a divisive figure among historians, thus gaining two juxtaposing nicknames: 'Master of the Field' and 'Butcher of the Somme'. The Battle of the Somme took place between 1 July and 18 November 1916 and is infamous for being the battle that incurred the most casualties in British military history.

Kelso Abbey

Kelso Abbey, founded in 1128 by monks of the Tironesian Order, is the oldest of the Borders abbeys, and was King David's base in southern Scotland. The remains of this abbey are less extensive than the three others, mostly due to a demolition in 1805. Only the west tower and transept remain.

Kelso Abbey was once one of the wealthiest abbeys in Scotland. Its huge estate contained Scotland's best-quality agricultural land and lucrative fisheries on the Tweed and Teviot rivers. However, it suffered the same fate as the other Borders abbeys and was burned and looted on several occasions.

Dryburgh Abbey: the burial place of Sir Walter Scott and Field Marshal Sir Douglas Haig (Stage 2)

Kelso Abbey was one of the wealthiest abbeys in Scotland (Stage 3)

King James II of Scotland (1430–1460) was killed within sight of Kelso Abbey during a battle that secured Scottish repossession of nearby Roxburgh Castle from the English. The abbey was the venue for the hasty coronation of the infant successor, King James III of Scotland (1451–1488), following the death of his father.

After falling into secular control after the Scottish Reformation in 1560, the abbey's estates were granted to Robert Ker of Cessford, an ancestor of the current Duke of Roxburghe, who resides at Floors Castle on the outskirts of Kelso. Several generations of Dukes of Roxburghe and members of their family are buried at the abbey.

Prince Henry of Scotland (1114–1152), son of King David I of Scotland, is also buried there. The Prince was also Earl of Northumberland from 1139 until his death.

Jedburgh Abbey

A priory at Jedburgh was founded by canons of the Augustinian Order in 1118, before the ascension of King David I to the Scottish throne; after which, it was raised to the status of abbey and gained extensive estate lands in both the Borders region and Northumberland. The abbey was a centre of political importance, its abbot being invited to attend Scottish Parliaments in Edinburgh.

In 1285 King Alexander III of Scotland (1241–1286) married Yolande of Dreux at the abbey, a union that emphasised Scottish independence from England due to Yolande's French lineage. Yolande was his second wife (his first wife, who died in 1275, was the daughter of King Henry III of England (1207–1272)). The royal wedding was attended by many nobles from France and Scotland. According to legend, a ghost appeared during the wedding, foretelling Alexander's death. The King died after falling from his horse while riding from his court at Edinburgh to join Yolande at Kinghorn in Fife, exactly a year after the premonition at their wedding.

Of all the Borders abbeys, Jedburgh was attacked the most often. The abbey was badly damaged

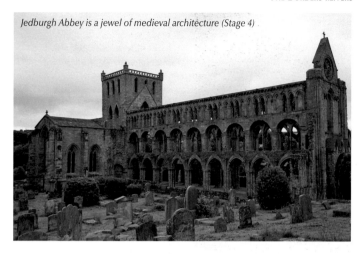

Jedburgh Abbey is a jewel of medieval architecture (Stage 4)

by English armies in 1297 as retribution for the victory of Sir William Wallace after his defeat of the Earl of Surrey at the Battle of Stirling Bridge. It was vandalised again by the English in 1346 after they had routed Scottish forces at the Battle of Neville's Cross near Durham. In 1410 and 1416 the abbey was attacked by forces loyal to the Duke of Albany, a ruthless Scottish politician and brother of King Robert III of Scotland (1390–1406). In 1464 it was targeted by the Earl of Warwick, and again in 1523 by the Earl of Surrey, when the abbey and Jedburgh town were set on fire. The seventh, and final, time the abbey was attacked was in 1544 by the forces of the Earl of Hertford. The ruins later became a Protestant parish kirk – an ignominious end for a Catholic abbey.

THE BORDERS REIVERS

The Borders reivers were notorious Scottish and English extended kinship groups active from the late 13th century until the beginning of the 17th century, although their heyday was during the 16th century. The word *reive* is an early English verb meaning 'to rob', which aptly describes the reivers' main source of livelihood. Loyalty to the family group was more important than nationality, and it was not uncommon for English and Scottish families of the same kin to join forces and carry out raids on both sides of the Border, despite border crossings being strictly illegal.

The Borders region had been devastated by the wars between the English and Scottish crowns and dependence on agriculture was not a secure option, as crops were often destroyed during the conflicts. In addition, much of the Borders region, prior to more recent extensive drainage, was a boggy place that was largely unsuited to raising crops. As a result, populations in the Borderlands were heavily reliant on livestock, which had the advantage of being mobile. The difficulty of surviving in this landscape, combined with political instability and a lack of governmental or royal authority, created conditions for gang warfare. Daily life, particularly during the Wars of Scottish Independence in the 14th century, and the so-called 'Rough Wooing of Scotland' in the 16th century, was extremely precarious, and the population depended on its wits to survive. The numerous ruined fortified tower houses we see in the Borders today are the legacy of those times. Anyone

living in or travelling through this region was at risk of attack, and it was as dangerous as any turbulent frontier region that exists in the world today.

Most of the time, reiving involved livestock and horse rustling, although kidnapping and extortion were also practised. The word 'blackmail' was coined during the time of the reivers and referred to protection money extorted from local populations. Winter was the main rustling season due to the long nights, and livestock was plump from spending the summer grazing. A counter-raid by the dispossessed to regain their herds and kinship honour was deemed mandatory and resulted in long-running feuds between groups of reivers.

Reivers were undoubtedly brave; they delighted in outwitting the border patrols and their tracking hounds.

Prior to extensive drainage, much of the Borders was a boggy place

Raids ranged from just a few men to several thousand, depending on the situation, and reivers risked execution if caught. Their courage and skill earned them a reputation as fearsome fighters, and they were often utilised as cavalry by both the English and Scottish authorities. Sometimes reivers were forced into serving the English or Scottish armies in lieu of a death sentence imposed on their families. Reivers were often overtly recalcitrant, however, and it was noted during the Battle of Ancrum Moor in 1545 that they changed sides mid battle.

A series of parliamentary acts brought the reivers and the subsequent Moss Troopers to heel. One of the most significant acts was passed in 1609, allowing for the prosecution of an Englishman in Scotland if a crime was committed there, or for a Scotsman to be tried in England for breaking the law on English soil.

There is no clear point in historical records that shows the decline of the reivers and the emergence of the Moss Troopers, who took their place as frontier brigands. Many Moss Troopers were armed deserters of the Wars of Three Kingdoms, a series of wars (including civil wars) between 1639 and 1653, involving the kingdoms of Ireland, England and Scotland. It seems that, unlike the reivers, the Moss Troopers were not groups of related kin. Despite the concerted efforts of the authorities, it was not until the early 18th century that the Borderlands finally became peaceful, when the remaining Moss Troopers were either executed or exiled to North America.

Some of the Borders reivers' kinship names are still common surnames in the Borders region today, and many Borderers are proud of their heritage. The reivers' legacy survives in the popular Common Ridings and festivals that take place throughout the region during the summer, when large groups of locals ride out on horseback to patrol their marches, or territorial boundaries. This ceremony has roots in the Borders Trysts, when the march (district) wardens would meet. These were the only times when reiving family groups from both sides of the border could legally mix and socialise.

COMMON RIDINGS AND LOCAL FESTIVALS

March	Hawick Reivers Festival
Early June	Hawick Common Riding
Mid June	Selkirk Common Riding
Mid/late June	Borders Book Festival, Melrose
Late June/early July	Jethart Callants Festival, Jedburgh (two weeks)
Late July	Kelso Civic Week (including Common Riding)

The months and locations of Common Ridings and local festivals are shown on page 21. The towns are lively during these events and accommodation should be booked well in advance.

AGRICULTURE AND COUNTRY ESTATES IN THE BORDERS

Until relatively recently it was thought that settled farming communities were first established in southern Scotland during the Neolithic Period, some 3,500–2,500 years ago. However, excavations at Cleave Dyke in Perthshire in 2000 revealed the remains of a farm that is thought to date from the Mesolithic Period, around 6,000 years ago. It is therefore possible that permanent farming settlements in the Borders lowlands first occurred at a similar time, potentially near the larger rivers (Tweed and Teviot).

During the Medieval Period, crops were grown on runrigs – strips of land that would be farmed on a rotational basis by the families of a village or town. Linen production was an important cottage industry in medieval times, and ethnobotanical studies have revealed that flax was planted in the Borders for that purpose. The upland areas, particularly the Cheviot Hills and the Southern Uplands, have long been used for sheep and cattle rearing, first practised on a large scale by shepherds and herdsmen employed by the Borders abbeys' estates. The woollen textile industry was very important to the Borders

The Borders has some of the best agricultural land in Scotland

economy from the Medieval Period to its decline in the 1980s. Borders towns – with the exception of Melrose – have suffered economically due to the demise of the woollen textile industry.

After the Scottish Reformation in 1560, extensive areas of former abbey lands were granted to local nobles, who built large mansions on their estates. In the early 17th century, a number of these estates planted woodlands to supply the huge national demand for timber, particularly for shipbuilding and construction. The estates' wealth further increased during the British Empire, when owners expanded their commercial interests. However, many of these estates became economically unsustainable due to staff shortages and taxation laws enacted after World War I. Some mansions have escaped demolition and are open to the public; they are certainly worth visiting if you have time.

Livestock droving – the transhumance of large flocks and herds over significant distances to markets – has existed in Britain since ancient times. The droving heyday was in the 19th century, when thousands of animals were driven south from the Borders and Highlands, sometimes as far as southern England. A drover required a permit, only granted if a man was over 30 years old and married. Droving declined and then ceased after the expansion of the railway network.

Farming, both livestock and arable, is still very important to the local economy, although, as with other regions in Britain, it now employs relatively few people. Commercial conifer forestry is replacing sheep farming as the main land use in some upland areas.

GEOLOGY AND NATURE

Geology
Around 450 million years ago, two continental plates collided, and the resulting uplift created the Southern Upland and the Cheviot ranges. The south-west to north-east orientation of these ranges reveals the angle of this collision. At that time the land that is now the Borders was an arid desert, evidenced today by the red soils created from ancient periodic river flows.

Between 400 and 360 million years ago, volcanic activity created hills such as Black Law, Rubers Law, the Minto Hills and the Cheviots. (The Eildon Hills were formed later.)

Many of these volcanic hills have a tapered extension orientated eastwards, caused by the erosive flow of ice sheets that scoured the area during successive ice ages. The rich soils that are found in the central and eastern Borders are the result of this erosion.

Nature
In the summer months you may see yellowhammers in country lanes, wood pigeons in fields and

Rubers Law, an ancient volcano (Stage 4)

woodlands, and wrens and blackbirds in woodlands. On field edges you may spot tortoiseshell butterflies and brown hares. You will certainly see buzzards and crows, perhaps in combat during the nesting seasons. On grassy upland slopes you might hear the trill of a skylark overhead or see the flash of the common blue butterfly on a breeze.

On the rivers you may see merganser or goosander ducks, herons, dippers, wagtails and oystercatchers. You may be lucky and spot an otter.

You might glimpse roe deer or badgers, although the best chance of spotting these elusive animals is while sitting quietly downwind of a woodland edge in the early morning or late evening.

Woodlands were historically used by farms as a resource for fuel wood

and fencing material production, but nowadays smaller farm woodlands are often unmanaged, or exist to provide windbreaks for crops and livestock, and for rearing pheasants. These woodlands provide an important habitat for insects, birds and flowers.

GETTING TO AND FROM THE BORDERS ABBEYS WAY

Tweedbank railway station is 600 metres from the official Borders Abbeys Way route but is the start of Stage 1 route description in this guide, as it is a popular access point for the Way. Galashiels Transport Interchange is the main transport hub for the area and is one stop from Tweedbank on the railway line. The Interchange is well served by long-distance and local buses and the Borders Railway.

By car

The Way can be accessed by car via the A68 from Edinburgh or Newcastle, the A72 from Glasgow, or the A7 from Edinburgh or Carlisle.

By train

The East Coast mainline connecting London, Newcastle and Edinburgh stops at Berwick-upon-Tweed, where regular buses depart for several towns on the Borders Abbeys Way. A train can also be taken from Edinburgh Waverley to Tweedbank railway terminus approximately every 30 minutes. The train also stops at Galashiels Transport Interchange.

Galashiels Transport Interchange has free toilet and shower facilities, a café, changing areas and locker facilities. Pay-and-display parking is available at a car park opposite. Tweedbank railway terminus has free parking, toilets and a hot food and drink outlet.

By bus

There are various bus services connecting the towns along the Borders Abbeys Way with Berwick-upon-Tweed railway station, Edinburgh, Carlisle and Newcastle. Most local and longer distance services are provided by Borders Buses. There are also services provided by Peter Hogg, Telford's Coaches and Scottish Borders Council (SBC). The relatively frequent local bus services allow for a return to the point of departure for people wanting to do stand-alone day walks, rather than walking the stages as a contiguous circuit. See Appendix C for detailed information on bus services.

If you plan on returning to your point of departure on the same day, it's best to get the bus to the end of the route stage and then walk back to your point of departure at your own pace.

Heading towards Melrose from Tweedbank station (Stage 1)

The Gattonside Footbridge (Stage 1)

WHERE TO STAY

Hotels and B&Bs

A choice of accommodation and facilities is available on each Stage of the Way and all the main settlements have B&B or hotel accommodation. Accommodation listed on airbnb.com or booking.com is not included in this guide, but may be a good alternative to the guesthouses, hotels or B&Bs listed in Appendix B, particularly in Newtown St Boswells and Selkirk, which have a more limited range of accommodation. It is recommended that you book accommodation in advance if you are walking in summer, particularly during the Common Ridings (see When to go and what to take for more information).

Camping

There are three campsites along the Way with the usual facilities. These are located at Melrose, Jedburgh and Hornshole, near Hawick. Ruberslaw Wild Camping is located between Jedburgh and Denholm, but there are no campers' facilities other than a field in which to pitch a tent. If you plan on camping while walking the entire route, you will need to wild camp some of the time. Wild camping is legal in Scotland, via the Land Reform (Scotland) Act 2003, although as a matter of courtesy it is still best to ask the landowner's permission if possible. Campers and walkers should follow the Scottish Outdoor Access Code, published

by Scottish Natural Heritage (SNH). Broadly speaking, this states that to enjoy Scotland's outdoors responsibly, you should:

- Take responsibility for your own actions
- Respect the interests of other people
- Care for the environment

See Appendix D for the SNH website and contact details.

MAPS AND PUBLIC ACCESS

Maps

The entire Borders Abbeys Way is waymarked in both directions. The Ordnance Survey (OS) maps covering the route are:

Stage	Landranger	Explorer
1	73	338, 339
2	74	339
3	74	339, OL16
4	80	331, OL16
5	79, 80	331, 338
6	73	338

The OS Landranger map series has a scale of 1:50,000 and the Explorer series has a scale of 1:25,000. This guide contains extracts of the OS Landranger map series overlaid with the route of the Borders Abbeys Way.

Explorer sheet 331 dated 2015 displays an incorrect Borders Abbeys Way route on Stage 4 (Jedburgh to Hawick). See Stage 4 map and route description in this book for the correct route information.

Public access

Scotland enjoys some of the best public access rights in the world and walkers have the right to roam the countryside with only a few restrictions. However, it is important to respect the Outdoor Access Code (see Camping, earlier). Follow any temporary footpath diversions made by landowners or the local authority and keep to the waymarked paths in fields planted with crops.

If you are walking with a dog, keep your dog on a short lead or at least under very close control. In bird breeding season (usually April–July) avoid disturbing ground-nesting birds. Cows with calves can become stressed and aggressive if a dog is present, so keep a safe distance and never pass between a mother and her calf with a dog. If a cow does charge, let go of the dog's lead, otherwise you may get injured by the cow. A cow will most likely pursue a dog and not you in this situation.

The Borders Abbeys Way is managed by Scottish Borders Council (SBC). If waymarkers are found to be damaged or missing, please inform the Countryside Access Officers at SBC. Contact details are in Appendix D. Mobile signal coverage is generally good on most of the Way.

WHEN TO GO AND WHAT TO TAKE

This route can be undertaken at any time of year, although walking between early spring and the end of autumn offers the chance of more settled weather, longer daylight hours and better walking conditions. That said, the maritime climate of Britain results in unpredictable weather, and conditions can change quickly.

It is recommended that you book accommodation in advance if walking in the summer months, and particularly during the Common Ridings (see The Borders reivers for when and where these take place). The towns are busy during these events.

If you are walking this route in summer, take both sun protection (including a hat and long-sleeved top) and insulating layers. You should carry waterproof layers in both summer

The W-shaped Borders Abbeys Way logo (in the middle)

The route is well waymarked

and winter. In winter you should also pack a warm hat, gloves and thermal underlayers.

Gaiters are also recommended. These may seem like a burden on a warm day in summer, but they will justify their weight in wet conditions. Good, waterproof walking boots and hiking socks are essential items. These should be lightweight boots in summer and leather boots in winter. Your comfort will make the difference between a pleasant walk and a miserable experience.

It is recommended that you pack 'second skin' gel plasters in case blisters occur. Failing that, adhesive bandages (or sticking plasters) will probably suffice. These can be bought at any pharmacy on the Way. Arnica pills or cream can reduce bruising caused by a twisted ankle or a fall. Arnica can be bought from most good health stores.

The route is well waymarked and you shouldn't get lost. The section across the southern flank of Black Law on Stage 4 is waymarked, but the path can be indistinct in places and may be difficult to follow in thick fog. It is therefore recommended that you also carry a map and compass or a GPS unit on this stage if poor weather is likely.

It is recommended that you drink sufficient water while walking on warm summer days. There are no obvious springs en route.

USING THIS GUIDE

A summary box at the start of each Stage displays information on the start and finish locations and their grid references, stage distance, approximate completion time, ascent, relevant OS maps and outline information on accommodation, refreshments en route and public transport to and from the stage. Facilities available on each Stage, contact information for accommodation on each Stage of the Way, bus service information and useful contacts are displayed in Appendices A, B, C and D, respectively.

A short introduction gives a brief overview of the stage, providing information on any major points of interest. Easily identifiable features that appear on OS maps are highlighted in bold throughout the route description to assist with navigation.

In addition to the abbeys there are various places of interest in each main settlement of the Way, such as museums and historic buildings. The locations of these places of interest are displayed on the town map on each route stage.

Distances and times

Larger distances are given in miles, with metric conversions. Distances of less than 1 kilometre are given only in metres. The walking time for each Stage has been calculated using Naismith's Rule: 3 miles per hour (4.8km per hour) plus ten minutes for every 100 metres of ascent. This calculation does not include any time for rests, photography, visiting sites of interest or admiring views.

GPX tracks

GPX tracks for the routes in this guidebook are available to download free at www.cicerone.co.uk/980/GPX. A GPS device is an excellent aid to navigation, but you should also carry a map and compass and know how to use them. GPX files are provided in good faith, but neither the author nor the publisher accepts responsibility for their accuracy.

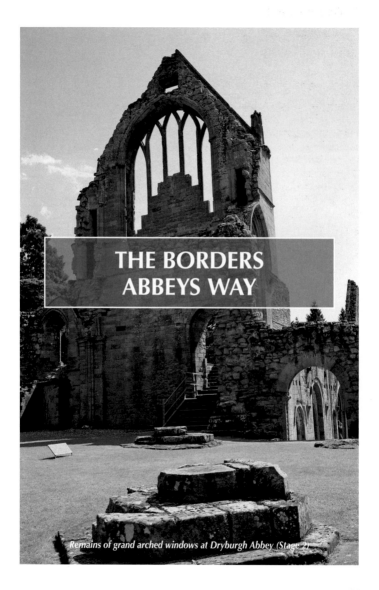

THE BORDERS
ABBEYS WAY

Remains of grand arched windows at Dryburgh Abbey (Stage 2)

31

STAGE 1

Tweedbank to Newtown St Boswells via Melrose

Start	Tweedbank railway station (NT 523 348)
Finish	Newtown St Boswells (Langlands Place; NT 576 318)
Distance	4.8 miles (7.7km)
Ascent	160m
Time	2hr
Maps	Landranger 73; Explorer 338 & 339
Refreshments	Pubs, shops, restaurants, cafés and takeaways in Melrose; café, takeaway, shops and hotel bar in Newtown St Boswells; takeaways, shop, café, restaurant, hotel restaurant and bar in St Boswells
Public transport	Trains approximately every 30 mins from Edinburgh to Tweedbank railway terminus (TWB) and Galashiels Transport Interchange. Regular buses to Galashiels Transport Interchange X95 from Edinburgh or Carlisle and 60 and 67 from Berwick-upon-Tweed (Borders Buses)

The first stage of the Borders Abbeys Way starts near Tweedbank railway terminus and continues to Newtown St Boswells via the popular and scenic town of Melrose. Melrose Abbey is undoubtedly the main attraction at Melrose, but there is also an interesting museum containing artefacts excavated from Trimontium Roman fort at nearby Newstead. The route is relatively flat and there are some pleasant views of the River Tweed. The section from Newstead to Newtown St Boswells is mostly on a road closed to public traffic. Alternative options to overnighting in Newtown St Boswells are either Melrose on Stage 1, Dryburgh Abbey Hotel or a B&B near Clintmains (Clint Lodge), both on Stage 2; or St Boswells (0.9 miles (1.5km)) off the Borders Abbeys Way.

Leaving Tweedbank railway terminus, cross the car park access road and continue along an asphalt cycle and walking path towards **Melrose**, waymarked as the Melrose Link Path.

> This section of path was once the **Waverley Route railway line**, connecting Edinburgh with Carlisle and was named after a series of novels by Sir Walter Scott. The railway, which opened in 1849, was constructed by the North British Railway. It was closed in 1969. The current Borders Railway from Edinburgh Waverley to Tweedbank was opened in 2015. It was the longest domestic railway track to be built in the UK for more than 100 years.

After 400 metres cross a minor road (Tweedside Park) and continue straight ahead, then bear left at a waymarker for the Southern Upland Way. (The Borders Abbeys Way shares the path with the Southern Upland Way until Gattonside Footbridge on the outskirts of Melrose.) Cross the busy B6374. ▶

Take care when crossing the B6374.

In front of you is a Borders Abbeys Way waypost indicating the route both to your right and to your left. Take the route to the right, passing through a wooden gate. A few metres beyond the gate, the River Tweed is visible on the left and there is an interpretation panel describing the events that took place at nearby Skirmish Hill.

Map continues on page 38

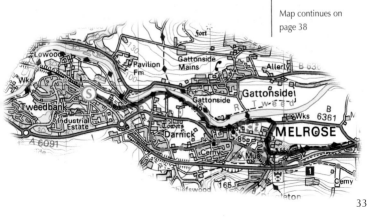

Skirmish Hill is named after an unsuccessful kidnap attempt on the 14-year-old King James V of Scotland (1512–1542) on 25 July 1526 by up to 600 men under the command of Walter Scott of Buccleuch. The young king fled to the safety of nearby Darnick Tower. The king, who was nephew of the English King Henry VIII, died at the age of 30 after the Battle of Solway Moss. His daughter Mary Stuart, Queen of Scots (1542–1587) succeeded him when she was just six days old.

Continue adjacent to the Tweed for 0.7 miles (1.2km), going through two gates to a minor road (Bleachfield) and some houses. Turn left, following the asphalt road. After 30 metres turn left again just before a small garage, as indicated by a Southern Upland Way waymarker, onto an unsurfaced track into woodland.

Shortly after, Gattonside Footbridge will come into view, with **Gattonside** visible on the opposite side of the River Tweed. The Southern Upland Way crosses the bridge, but the Borders Abbeys Way remains on the southern bank of the Tweed. ◀

It is highly likely that the Earl of Hertford sited his cannons at Gattonside when his army bombarded Melrose Abbey in 1544.

The River Tweed flows east to Berwick

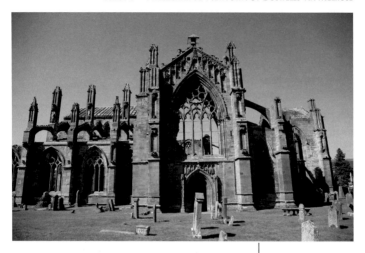

The Way continues into parkland on the outskirts of Melrose. Some picnic benches here make a handy spot to eat a packed lunch. Alternatively, there is a wide variety of refreshments in Melrose. Near the benches a waymarker indicates Melrose town centre to the right, and the Southern Upland Way straight on. (Although there is no Borders Abbeys Way waymarker.)

To reach the town centre via **Melrose Abbey**, continue along the Borders Abbeys Way (and Southern Upland Way) adjacent to the Tweed.

Passing the Gattonside Footbridge, the path becomes an asphalt track and then a minor road (Chain Bridge Road). Melrose Rugby Football Club is visible to the left. Shortly after the rugby club, Melrose Abbey will be visible at a T-junction. Cross the road (Annay Road) and turn right, continuing on the pavement towards the abbey.

The Way continues past the abbey and turns left into a park adjoining the abbey's iron-railed fence. Continue through the park and then cross a small footbridge. When the path enters a suburban street (Priorsdene), continue straight ahead on the pavement. After 190 metres the street curves to the right just after a row of garages on

Melrose Abbey was once on the main route between Edinburgh and England and provided travellers with lodgings and food

MELROSE

Melrose is a very popular small town and there is a wide choice of accommodation (see Appendix B for details) and places to eat. The abbey is the main attraction, and its museum houses the largest collection of medieval artefacts in Scotland.

Harmony Garden (Apr–Oct daily 10am–5pm) is a pleasant walled garden opposite the abbey. It is free and open to the public, and hosts the Borders Book Festival in June every year. Reserve accommodation well in advance if staying in Melrose during the book festival.

Priorwood Garden (Apr–Oct daily 10am–5pm), a National Trust for Scotland property dedicated to the art of dried flower arranging, is located on Abbey Road, just to the south of the abbey.

The town is at the base of the Eildon Hills, three distinctive peaks just to the south of the town. The nearby **Roman fort** (Trimontium), at the village of **Newstead**, was named after these hills. However, it is very difficult to see any evidence of the fort at the 370-acre site. The Trimontium Trust manages The Three Hills Roman Heritage Centre (Apr–Oct Mon–Sat 10.30am–4.30pm), which is located in Market Square and serves as a tourist information centre. The museum displays items found at the site, including coin hoards, jewellery and a reconstruction of an AD first- or second-century Roman soldier's head, based on a skull found during the construction of the Waverley railway line. The soldier was found at the bottom of a Roman-era well and had probably been murdered.

Harmony Garden, opposite Melrose Abbey

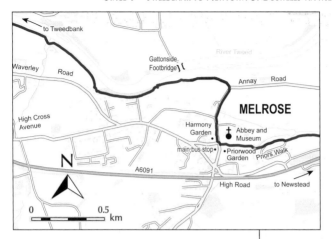

the left. At the curve the Borders Abbeys Way leaves the street to the left, running along the top of a steep-sided bank. Continue straight ahead, ignoring the path to the right (to Newstead). The Way eventually emerges next to some stables and a parking area.

Turn left onto an asphalt road (Dean Road) just beyond the stables on the outskirts of the village of **Newstead**, and continue downhill for 50 metres. ▶ The

Newstead claims to be the oldest continuously inhabited village in Scotland, dating to at least AD650. In medieval times, the village housed stonemasons who worked at Melrose Abbey.

Leaving Newstead under a verdant canopy

37

Way then turns right next to a house (Mill Cottage) and continues uphill via a woodland track, under a tangle of branches and foliage.

The track emerges onto an asphalt path. Turn right at the waymarker before you enter the suburban street visible ahead, to go under a former railway line and an underpass of the A6091. When the path emerges at the south side of the A6091 it turns right then doubles back to the left through galvanised gates. Turn right just after the gates, heading uphill towards the distinctive Eildon Hills on a field access track between high hedges. Turn left when the track emerges onto an asphalt road at the base of the Eildon Hills. ◀

The road is closed to vehicles beyond the metal gates a few metres uphill. About 50 metres uphill of the gates is the **Rhymer's Stone** and a viewpoint providing expansive views to the north.

The Romans used the highest peak of the Eildon Hills as a signal station. Prior to that a Bronze Age fort belonging to the Votadini tribe occupied the site.

The Rhymer's Stone is where the fabled **Eildon Tree** once grew. It was under this tree that Thomas the Rhymer took a nap and disappeared to the land of elves. He then returned to nearby Earlston for a further seven years, before disappearing for good, presumably back to Elfland. Born in 1220, Thomas became well known for his many accurate prophesies, including the building of the Leaderfoot Viaduct which carried the Waverley Route railway over the River Tweed centuries after his disappearance.

A little further ahead there is an option to walk up the steep Eildon Hills via waymarked paths on your right. This is a detour from the Borders Abbeys Way, but fantastic panoramic views are the reward.

Continue on the minor road, passing the hamlet of **Eildon** (waymarked, but not visible from the road) to a road junction. Turn left to enter **Newtown St Boswells**. Cross the street (B6398) to the opposite pavement and turn right. The street becomes Langlands Place.

Monument to Thomas the Rhymer

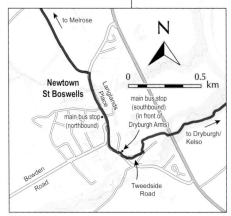

Alternative ending at St Boswells:
To continue to **St Boswells** 2 miles (3.1km) to the south-east, 0.9 miles (1.5km) off the Borders Abbeys Way, follow Stage 2 as far as the Dryburgh

NEWTOWN ST BOSWELLS

Newtown St Boswells was once an important centre for milling grain and livestock sales and export. Its railway closed in 1969, after which the village suffered economically. Eating out is limited to the Dryburgh Arms Hotel and a café in Milestone Garden Centre (daily 9am–5pm). For a wider choice, you could walk to St Boswells either via the Borders Abbeys Way (as far as the Dryburgh Footbridge and then follow St Cuthbert's Way from there (see Stage 2 map)) or along a well-lit pavement next to the A68 for 0.7 miles (1.2km). In St Boswells there is an Italian restaurant (Hunter's Stables; Wed–Mon for lunch and dinner) and a café (Main Street Trading Company; Tue–Sat 9am–5pm/4pm Sun), and the four-star Buccleuch Arms Hotel, which has a restaurant and serves bar meals. There are also two takeaways in St Boswells. See Appendix A for a summary of facilities.

Footbridge. Do not cross the bridge but continue on the south side of the River Tweed, following the St Cuthbert's Way waymarkers.

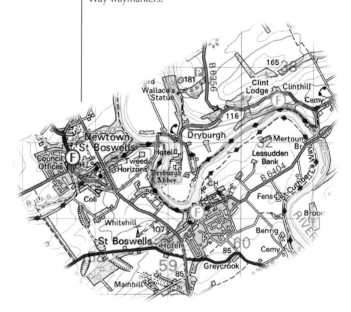

STAGE 2
Newtown St Boswells to Kelso

Start	Newtown St Boswells (NT 576 318; Langlands Place)
Finish	Kelso (NT 727 339; The Square)
Distance	15 miles (24.2km)
Ascent	302m
Time	5hr 30min
Maps	Landranger 74; Explorer 339
Refreshments	Pub, shops, takeaways, restaurants and café in St Boswells, 0.9 miles (1.5km) off route; restaurant at Dryburgh Abbey Hotel (next to Dryburgh Abbey); pubs, takeaways, shops, restaurants and cafés in Kelso
Public transport	Buses link Newtown St Boswells with: St Boswells, Jedburgh, Melrose, Edinburgh, Berwick-upon-Tweed, Kelso, Galashiels Transport Interchange and Tweedbank railway station

After leaving Newtown St Boswells, Stage 2 passes through a wooded glen adjacent to the River Tweed, which has been identified as an ancient semi-natural woodland site by Scottish Natural Heritage (SNH). The Way then crosses a footbridge to Dryburgh Abbey and continues to Kelso via the hamlet of Clintmains (B&B available) on minor roads, farm tracks and riverside paths. This is the longest stage of the Way, but it is relatively flat. Most of the road walking occurs after Clintmains. A bus can be caught to Kelso (service 67, Borders Buses) from a bus stop at the junction of Clintmains road end and the B6404 if you'd rather avoid the Clintmains to Kelso section. Buses are approximately every two hours. There is no timetable in the bus shelter. Timetables are on the Borders Buses website: www.bordersbuses.co.uk.

To re-join the route from St Boswells:
If Stage 1 was completed at St Boswells rather than Newtown St Boswells, you will need to backtrack to the Dryburgh Footbridge to continue on the route.

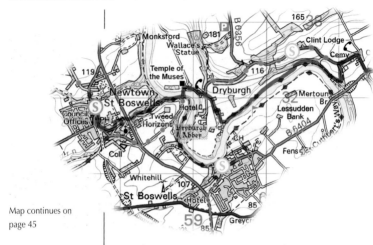

Map continues on
page 45

To continue
from Newtown St Boswells:
Continue along Langlands Place, passing the village
newsagents, and turn left at the Dryburgh Arms Hotel
onto Tweedside Road.

Near the end of Tweedside Road, turn left, as indicated by a waymarker, going behind the back of some
houses (this is also a section of St Cuthbert's Way heading
to St Boswells). Continue downhill on the asphalt lane to
a bridge that carries the A68 overhead.

Just under the bridge the path leaves the asphalt track
to the right, heading into woodland. Continue on this
path along south bank of the Tweed for 900 metres until
you reach the Dryburgh Footbridge. Cross the bridge to
the north bank of the Tweed and turn right.

Dryburgh Suspension Bridge was first built in 1817
to replace a ferry service at the same location. It
was the first chain suspension bridge to be built in
Scotland but was destroyed by a gale in 1818. A
subsequent bridge collapsed. The current bridge,
suspended from cables rather than chains, was built
in 1872.

Dryburgh Suspension Bridge spans the River Tweed

The path joins an estate track (Dryburgh Mains). Just to the left of this path junction is a gate and a path leading uphill to the Temple of the Muses. ▸

Continue past some large houses and an estate wall for 600 metres, then turn right at the road junction a few metres beyond some white terraced cottages. Pass the driveway to **Dryburgh Abbey Hotel** and continue to the entrance of **Dryburgh Abbey** (public toilets available just past the abbey entrance).

The neoclassical Temple of the Muses was erected in 1818 as a tribute to local poet James Thomson, who wrote the words to 'Rule, Britannia!'

Temple of The Muses

43

DRYBURGH ABBEY

The Dryburgh Yew is situated within the abbey grounds. The yew is said to have been planted by the abbey monks and is more than 900 years old. It could be the oldest tree in the Borders. With its lawned surroundings and grand old trees, Dryburgh is perhaps the most peaceful and atmospheric of the four ruined abbeys.

The ruins of Dryburgh Abbey are allegedly haunted by a ghost of a small man wearing iron boots. Apparently, this spirit is associated with a hermit woman who resided in a ruined vault at the abbey after the Jacobite uprising in 1745. According to Sir Walter Scott, who recorded Borders legends and ballads, the benevolent ghost would tidy the woman's belongings when she was out of the room. The ghost's choice of footwear is a mystery.

The ruined cloister of Dryburgh Abbey

The Way continues past the abbey and down a wide track flanked by tall trees. Turn left near the end of the track, going over a stile. The path continues on a grassy path adjacent to a walled garden. The River Tweed becomes visible to the right of the track, with St Boswells golf course on the south side of the river.

The River Tweed is one of the most prestigious salmon fishing rivers in Scotland. Some beats (stretches of river) cost up to £4,000 per rod per week. During medieval times, the fishing rights were controlled by abbey monks.

The Way then joins an unsurfaced vehicle track and enters some woodland, gaining height above the Tweed. When the vehicle track veers left, the Way continues straight ahead through a kissing gate into a field on top of a small riverside cliff, before passing into another small woodland.

A few metres inside the woodland is a three-fingered waypost where you turn left and head uphill on a track. The track joins a minor road (B6356) next to the entrance to a graveyard. ▸

Turn right onto the road and continue for a few hundred metres to the hamlet of **Clintmains** (B&B and evening meals available at Clint Lodge, see Appendix B), where the road veers downhill to the right and leads to a T-junction at the B6404. Turn left onto the grassy verge and pass a small wooden bus shelter. (Borders Buses service 67 stops here.) You can take the bus from here to Kelso if you are walking the route in a clockwise direction, or to St Boswells, Melrose or Galashiels if walking the route in an anticlockwise direction.

To go to Clint Lodge B&B, turn left onto the road and continue along it for 600 metres.

Map continues on page 47

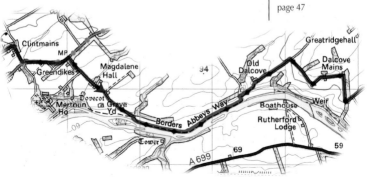

Passing through Clintmains

Beware drain holes hidden beneath grass at the edge of the B6404.

Cross the B6404 with caution to the opposite (south) side of the road at the waymarker just beyond the bus shelter. Continue on the roadside verge heading east for 300 metres, then turn right onto a farm access track. ◄

About 10 metres down the track turn left onto a woodland path adjacent to the B6404. At the end of the path turn right onto a minor road and continue for 800 metres past **Magdalene Hall** and some estate cottages. The road becomes a field access track and passes through a small car park before continuing adjacent to the River Tweed for 1 mile (1.6km). It then passes through a gate and gains height on a vehicle track, passing a house (**Old Dalcove**). About 900 metres after the gate you will reach a minor road where you turn right, heading downhill. The road swings to the left and passes farm buildings (**Dalcove Mains**).

At the road end turn right onto a grassy track. After 0.9 miles (1.5km), the track emerges onto a minor road with a row of estate cottages on your left, just past **Manorhill Farm**. Turn left, heading uphill on the road; then turn right after 400 metres.

Continue for 800 metres and turn left then right, passing **Haymount Farm** on a straight minor road heading east for 1 mile (1.6km) to a crossing of the busy B6397.

Continue straight ahead past a low white building on a farm access road heading off the B6397. The Way leaves the access road on a narrow grassy lane just before the access road bears right towards farm buildings (**Wester Muirdean**).

The grassy lane emerges at the A6089, where you cross the road and continue straight ahead along a minor road and then

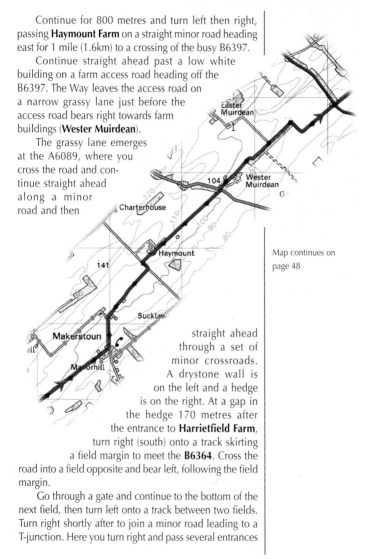

Map continues on page 48

straight ahead through a set of minor crossroads. A drystone wall is on the left and a hedge is on the right. At a gap in the hedge 170 metres after the entrance to **Harrietfield Farm**, turn right (south) onto a track skirting a field margin to meet the **B6364**. Cross the road into a field opposite and bear left, following the field margin.

Go through a gate and continue to the bottom of the next field, then turn left onto a track between two fields. Turn right shortly after to join a minor road leading to a T-junction. Here you turn right and pass several entrances

The name Kelso is derived from *Calkou* (Old Welsh for 'chalky outcrop'), which pre-dates the town. The town was established when the abbey was built.

to **Kelso Racecourse**. Follow the road until it joins Golf Course Road in Kelso. ▶

Kelso has the illustrious claim of being the departure point of **the world's first international flight**. In 1785 the celebrated Italian hot air balloonist Vincenzo Lunardi (1754–1806) took off from the Knowes (now a car park) and landed in northern England.

Cross Golf Road and turn left, continuing for 250 metres until opposite the indoor ice rink. Here you turn right down an asphalt track between garden fences, heading south. The Way then swings to the right, with

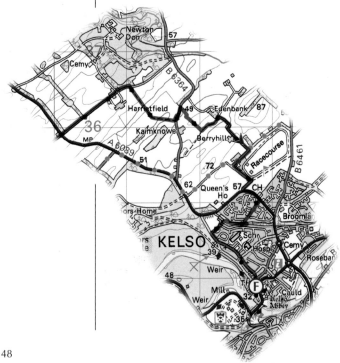

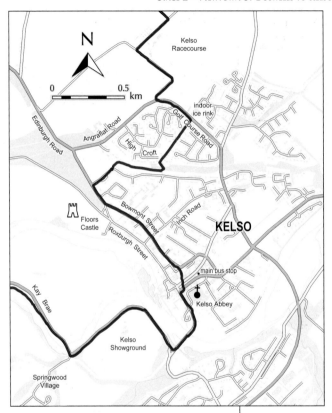

lawned areas each side of the path, until meeting Croft Road. At the end of Croft Road turn left onto Edinburgh Road, which becomes Bowmont Street.

Just past Kelso Library, Bowmont Street curves to the left. At the curve cross the road and go through a narrow entrance to Market Square. Kelso Abbey is on Bridge Street, leading off Market Square. You will see the ruins rising above shops about half way down Bridge Street.

Kelso Abbey is the burial place of generations of Dukes of Roxburghe

If you have time to spend a day in Kelso, **Floors Castle** (28 Apr–1 Oct daily 11am–5pm) is worth a visit. Despite its name it is actually a mansion rather than a fortress and is Scotland's largest inhabited house. Built in the 1720s, it is home to the Duke of Roxburghe, whose family has been associated with Roxburghshire since the 12th century. The mansion is open to the public and contains some impressive tapestries and other works of art. There are self-guided walking routes around the estate grounds, as well as two cafés and a walled garden.

STAGE 3
Kelso to Jedburgh

Start	Kelso (NT 727 339; Market Square)
Finish	Jedburgh (NT 650 205; Abbey Place)
Distance	13.5 miles (21.7km)
Ascent	268m
Time	5hr
Maps	Landranger 74; Explorer 339 and OL16
Refreshments	Pubs, shops, takeaways, restaurants and cafés in Jedburgh
Public transport	Buses link Kelso with: St Boswells, Newtown St Boswells, Hawick, Denholm, Jedburgh, Melrose, Selkirk, Edinburgh, Berwick-upon-Tweed, Galashiels Transport Interchange and Newcastle upon Tyne

This stage of the route follows the course of the River Teviot and then Jed Water to Jedburgh. The route passes the remains of Roxburgh Castle, once one of the most important fortifications in southern Scotland, and through the hamlet of Roxburgh (no facilities available). This stage is relatively flat and includes a pleasant mix of riverside paths, a section of former railway and a short section of Dere Street, a Roman road that once connected York with Scotland. There are some impressive views of the undulating central Borders countryside and the approach into Jedburgh passes below some picturesque sandstone cliffs.

From Market Square, walk south along Bridge Street and past **Kelso Abbey**, where Bridge Street veers to the right and crosses the River Tweed via Kelso Bridge.

> **Kelso Bridge** was originally built in 1754 and replaced a ferry service at the same location that was often dangerous in times of high water. The current bridge was built in 1803 after the original bridge collapsed. The building at the northern end was once a tollhouse. The price of the tolls caused riots in 1854.

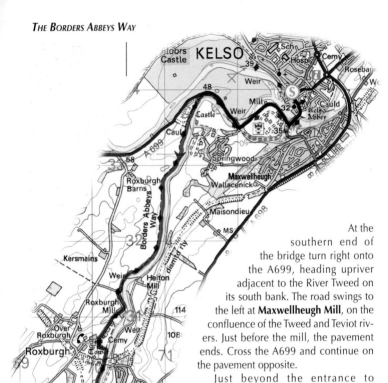

Map continues on page 54

At the southern end of the bridge turn right onto the A699, heading upriver adjacent to the River Tweed on its south bank. The road swings to the left at **Maxwellheugh Mill**, on the confluence of the Tweed and Teviot rivers. Just before the mill, the pavement ends. Cross the A699 and continue on the pavement opposite.

Just beyond the entrance to Springwood Village (a private retirement complex), cross the bridge and continue along the pavement. At the end of the pavement, cross the wall via a stone stile. Here you will find an interpretation panel providing information on the now vanished medieval village of Roxburgh.

The village of **Roxburgh** was once King David I of Scotland's de facto capital. In the Middle Ages its importance rivalled Edinburgh, Stirling, Perth and Berwick-upon-Tweed. It suffered greatly during the Scottish Wars of Independence and was destroyed in 1460 by Scottish forces, along with nearby Roxburgh Castle, when they captured it from the English.

Looking east to Kelso Bridge. The old tollhouse is visible on the left.

ROXBURGH CASTLE

Roxburgh Castle was built in 1125 by King David I of Scotland and was of huge strategic importance due to its location on a promontory between the Tweed and Teviot rivers. The castle was occupied by both English and Scottish forces at various times. In 1460, King James II of Scotland was killed by one of his own cannons, which exploded during an assault to capture the castle from the English.

Roxburgh Castle was once known as *Marchidun*, meaning 'Cavalry Fort' in Old Welsh, a Celtic language spoken in the Borders from the early ninth century to the early 12th century. No archaeological excavations have ever been permitted at the site, although there is some speculation that its Celtic name is indicative of an earlier Roman fort. A hoard of Roman-era coins has been found at nearby Springwood Park.

Turn to the right, heading upriver on the bank of the River Teviot. ▶ After about 800 metres you will pass the remains of Roxburgh Castle, visible at the top of a steep bank.

Continue along the riverside path for 1.7 miles (2.7km) to a small green hut. Go over the adjacent stile to join a minor tarmac road and turn left. The road passes

Fishermen's shelters along the riverbank make handy spots for a snack. Here you might spot herons and mergansers.

through a small farmyard (**Roxburgh Mill**) and continues towards the hamlet of **Roxburgh** (no facilities available).

Turn left onto an asphalt track just after the graveyard and follow the track past some houses, bearing left after 120 metres onto an unsurfaced field access track. In the field opposite is **Wallace's Tower**, a ruined 16th-century *pele* tower that once belonged to the Kerr reiving family (ancestors of the Duke of Roxburghe). The track turns to the right as it emerges at the riverbank and continues upriver under Roxburgh Viaduct.

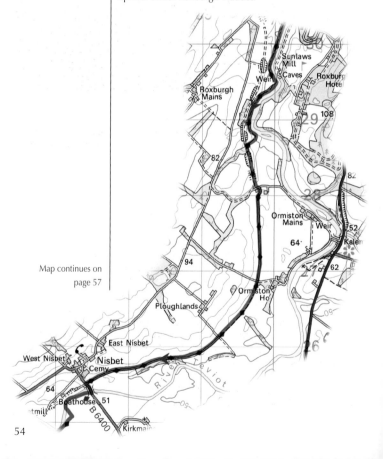

Map continues on page 57

About 900 metres after the viaduct it is possible to see **Sunlaws Caves** on the opposite bank of the river. The caves are said to have sheltered Bonnie Prince Charlie's horses in 1745, during his march from Jedburgh to Kelso.

Roxburgh Viaduct once carried a branch of the Waverley Line

One and a half miles (2.2km) beyond the viaduct, the path veers to the right, away from the river and into a field. Follow the field edge, adjacent to a drystone wall. At the end of the wall cross the stile to go up some wooden steps and turn left onto a disused railway line.

After following the former railway for 560 metres, descend the steps to a minor tarmac road opposite the former Kirkbank station (now a house) and turn left onto the tarmac road, then turn right onto a track skirting behind the former station to continue on the disused railway line. The Way continues for 2.5 miles (4km) until it joins an asphalt road (B6400) just south of the hamlet of **Nisbet** (no facilities available) at the former railway station. ▸

Nisbet has been designated a Conservation Area by Scottish Borders Council. Its appearance has changed little since the 19th century.

Turn left onto the asphalt road (B6400) at the former Nisbet Railway Station (now Riverside Cottage) and cross the road bridge over the River Teviot. At the southern end of the bridge turn right into a field and continue along the riverbank, following the Teviot upriver and then follow the fence as it swerves to the left. Cross the stile over the fence and continue along the grassy track for 580 metres.

Turn left at the waypost on a grassy track leading away from the river, and then right at the next waypost. After 210 metres you will come to a path junction, where you turn left. After 830 metres the path meets the busy A698. Here you turn right and continue for 80 metres on the verge, before crossing the road at the waymarker. ◀

Cross the A698 with caution due to fast traffic.

Continue along the minor asphalt road leading off the A698 and head uphill on the stony track leading off to the left. This section of path is waymarked as the Borders Abbeys Way, St Cuthbert's Way and Dere Street.

Dere Street was a Roman road that ran from York to Edinburgh and possibly to Perth. The modern A68 and A1 follow some sections of the Roman road. The Roman name of the route is lost. Its modern English name is derived from the post-Roman Anglo Saxon kingdom of Deira, which was traversed by part of the route.

Fishing on the River Teviot

Follow Dere Street for 920 metres until a Borders Abbeys Way waymarker, where you turn to the right. This spot provides some impressive views of the Eildon Hills and the Waterloo Monument. ▸

After 800 metres the path joins a minor asphalt road at **Mount Ulston**, a large house. Continue downhill to a junction with another minor road. Turn left at the junction and continue for 550 metres until you come to the A68 at the edge of **Jedburgh**.

Cross the A68 and continue through parkland on an asphalt path adjacent to Jed Water, passing a scenic sandstone cliff on the opposite side of the river. The path then joins an asphalt road (Old Bongate). After 85 metres turn right, crossing the bridge over Jed Water. Shortly after you will arrive at a junction with the High Street. Here you can turn right and continue up the High Street to the town centre (Market Place) or continue on the more circuitous official route.

The Waterloo Monument was built between 1817 and 1824 to commemorate the Battle of Waterloo. A previous monument on the site collapsed.

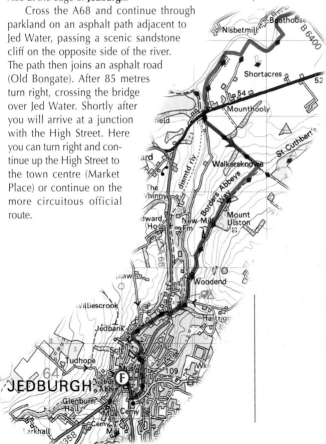

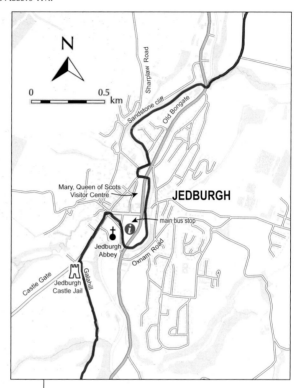

To follow the official route, turn left at the junction with the High Street and continue on the path passing under the A68. Turn right and continue for 635 metres adjacent to Jed Water. The path goes under the A68 again and emerges onto Abbey Place, where you will find **Jedburgh Abbey**

Beautiful arched windows at Jedburgh Abbey

JEDBURGH

A day spent in Jedburgh is certainly worthwhile if you have time. Jedburgh Abbey was once defended by French military; excavations have revealed their cannon embankments. Within the abbey's grounds are the remains of ancillary buildings where the monks ate and slept, as well as a large kitchen and cellar, which provide tantalising evidence of medieval daily monastic life. The abbey's visitor centre contains a display of artefacts found at the abbey during excavations, including early Christian artefacts that pre-date the abbey, and a walrus ivory comb.

Celtic carving on display at Jedburgh Abbey

Jedburgh Castle Jail (21 Mar–1 Nov Mon–Sat 10am–4.30pm, Sun 1–4pm; free admission) was built in 1823 in a castellated style on the site of a former castle, demolished in 1409. It is now a museum containing original prison blocks, providing an insight into the Georgian penal system, as well as the history of the town.

Mary, Queens of Scots Visitor Centre (30 Mar–1 Nov daily 9.30am–4.30pm; free admission), is situated within a 16th-century tower house on Queen Street. Mary Stuart was executed at Fotheringhay Castle in 1587 on the orders of her cousin, Queen Elizabeth I of England. This led to a series of raids across the Border into England by enraged Scottish nobles and their cohorts. Mary stayed in Jedburgh in 1566 and this homage to the tragic queen contains a lock of her hair, her death mask and exquisite 17th-century embroidery.

The interior of Jedburgh Abbey

STAGE 4
Jedburgh to Hawick

Start	Jedburgh (NT 650 205; Abbey Place)
Finish	Hawick (NT 505 153; Teviotdale Leisure Centre)
Distance	13.1 miles (21.1km)
Ascent	547m
Time	5hr 15min
Maps	Landranger 80; Explorer 331 and OL16
Refreshments	Pubs, shops, takeaways, restaurants and cafés in Hawick; pubs, café, Italian restaurant and village shop in Denholm
Public transport	Buses link Jedburgh with: St Boswells, Newtown St Boswells, Hawick, Denholm, Melrose, Selkirk, Edinburgh, Kelso, Galashiels Transport Interchange and Newcastle upon Tyne

The route climbs steeply after leaving Jedburgh, then climbs at a gentler gradient before another steeper climb to the southern flank of Black Law (338m). On a clear day the panoramic views from the summit of Black Law – a short distance uphill from the Way – are a just reward for the short diversion. Although it is waymarked, the path on Black Law is indistinct in places and may be difficult to follow in fog. From Black Law the Way leads to the picturesque village of Denholm, ideally placed for lunch halfway between Jedburgh and Hawick. There are also B&Bs available. From Denholm the Way follows the northern bank of the River Teviot upriver to Hawick, the largest town on the Borders Abbey Way. The section from Denholm to Hawick is flat.

From Abbey Place head uphill for 350 metres on Castlegate to the Castle Jail and Museum. At the jail entrance turn left onto Galahill, skirting the walls of the museum. After a short ascent, the asphalt road descends, becoming a stony track. At the bottom of the track bear left at the waymarker onto the footpath.

Map continues on
page 64

The Way continues up some wooden steps and becomes a grassy track, then joins an asphalt track at **Todlaw Farm**. Turn right 300 metres beyond the farm, heading uphill on a grassy lane bounded by hedges and trees.

At the top of the lane turn left and continue on the farm track for 1.2 miles (1.9km). Turn right at a stile, heading down some wooden steps to a small gulley, then steeply uphill along the edge of a field. At the top of the hill turn left, going through a wooden gate. A few metres ahead the path leads onto an open hillside just past a woodland strip. The summit of **Black Law**, topped with phone masts, is uphill and to the right, a short distance from the Way. ◄

In low visibility, the waymarkers on Black Law may not be visible and you could lose your way. It is recommended that you have a map and compass or a GPS unit as backup if the forecast is for poor weather.

Follow the waymarkers across the open hillside, with some grand views of Rubers Law, an ancient volcano to the south-west. The Way then descends steeply adjacent

to a wooded gulley (Blacklaw Strip). Continue down the edge of the woodland; just beyond it, the path goes through a gap in a hawthorn hedge and turns left to follow a drystone wall. After 300 metres go through a gate and turn right onto a farm track heading downhill to a minor asphalt road.

Turn left onto the asphalt road and then right at the T-junction a few metres ahead, descending to cross a bridge. At **Sawmill Cottage**, just after the bridge, turn left uphill on the road towards Bonchester Bridge.

Heading downhill from Black Law

OS Explorer sheet 331 dated 2015 displays an incorrect Borders Abbeys Way route at this point. In addition, the waymarker opposite Sawmill Cottage may be obscured by vegetation. Beware of going the wrong way here!

After 240 metres the road swings to the left. The path leaves the road just before the curve and heads uphill on a farm track to enter woodland. Turn left at the junction a few metres inside the woodland and follow the track for 140 metres before going over a stile into a field. Follow the field edge to the right, next to a wire fence with trees on the other side, to a waymarker attached to the fence. Turn left here as indicated, and follow the wall for 340 metres, before crossing the wall into another field via a stile.

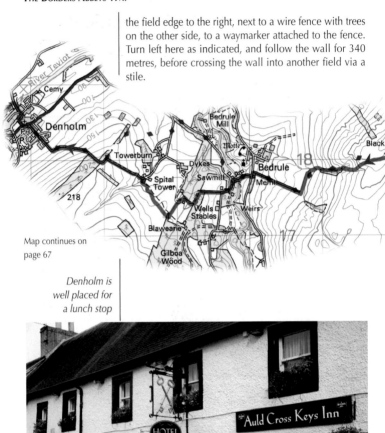

Map continues on page 67

Denholm is well placed for a lunch stop

64

DENHOLM

Denholm is a quaint village and a designated Conservation Area, due to the unique green at the centre of the village and the distinctive architecture – it is a planned village, dating to 1664. Denholm has accommodation (see Appendix B), two good pubs, a café and an Italian restaurant.

In the centre of Denholm village green is a commemorative monument to Dr John Leyden in the style of a Gothic spire. Born in Denholm in 1775 (d. 1811), Dr Leyden was a talented orientalist scholar who became Professor of Hindustani at Calcutta, where he later became a judge. Along with Lord Minto and Sir Stamford Raffles, Leyden was instrumental in the founding of Singapore. He died of an illness at the age of 36 in Batavia (present-day

Monument to Dr John Leyden on Denholm Village Green

Java), Indonesia. The monument also commemorates his descendant, John Lamb Leyden (1904–1988).

Buses can be taken from opposite the Auld Cross Keys Inn to Hawick, Kelso or Jedburgh daily, around every two hours (service 20, Peter Hogg and Borders Buses) until about 6pm.

Cross the field and go over another stile. After 400 metres the Way joins an unsurfaced farm track at some buildings (**Spital Tower** on OS maps). Turn left onto this track, heading uphill past Ruberslaw Wild Camping.

At the top of the hill, turn left and continue for 70 metres adjacent to a woodland strip before turning right. Go through the gate and head downhill on the track to **Denholm**, where the track emerges onto a sub-urban street (The Loaning). Turn left at the end of The Loaning into the main village street (A698).

John Leyden's birthplace, the thatched Leyden Cottage, is on Leyden Road.

Cross the main street (A698) with caution and continue next to the village green on the road (Kirkside), opposite the Fox and Hounds pub. The road swings to the right, becoming Leyden Road. ◀ After a few metres, turn left at the junction and continue downhill on the **B6405** to a small

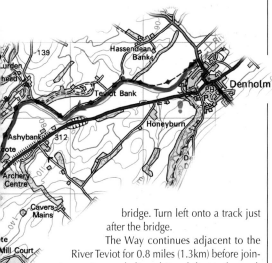

bridge. Turn left onto a track just after the bridge.

The Way continues adjacent to the River Teviot for 0.8 miles (1.3km) before joining a minor asphalt road. Turn left onto the road, which parallels the river, and continue for 0.9 miles (1.5km) until a waymarker indicating a left turn off the road just before Knowetown Cottages.

The Way continues next to the River Teviot through woodland for 1.3 miles (2km), before emerging onto a minor asphalt road at Hornshole Bridge.

There is no waymarker at Hornshole Bridge. Continue west along the road and do not cross the bridge.

Eighty metres after the bridge, the Way turns left at a waymarker onto an unsurfaced woodland path adjacent to the River Teviot and continues for 1 mile (1.6km) before joining an asphalt road on the outskirts of Hawick. Go past Hawick's rugby ground and football pitch to a roundabout where you bear left onto a suburban road (Mansfield Road).

To continue to the town centre, walk beyond the large roundabout at the end of Mansfield Road. A footbridge spans the River Teviot near the traffic lights. Cross this bridge and continue on North Bridge Street to the High Street.

Hawick High Street

HAWICK

Hawick was originally named in Old Welsh as *Hagawic* (a settlement surrounded by a hedge). It is the second largest town in the Scottish Borders (Galashiels is the largest) and, like the other towns in the area, it relied on the woollen textile industry for its economic well-being. Since the closure of the mills the town's economy has suffered, and its population has decreased in more recent years.

The oldest surviving building is 16th-century Drumlanrig's Tower, now home to the Borders Textile Towerhouse (Apr–Oct Mon–Sat 10am–4.30pm, Sun 12–3pm; Nov–Mar Mon and Wed–Sat 10am–4pm; free admission), celebrating the Borders' textile industry. It also houses Hawick's tourist information centre and a café.

The recently enhanced Hawick Museum at Wilton Lodge Park is worth a visit if you plan on spending a day in Hawick (Apr–Sept Mon–Fri 10am–12pm, 1–5pm, Sat–Sun 2–5pm; Oct–Mar Mon–Fri 12–3pm, Sun 1–3pm; free admission). The Lodge hosts a changing programme of art and museum exhibitions, and the pleasant estate surrounding the lodge contains a walled garden, fountains, floral displays and mature trees.

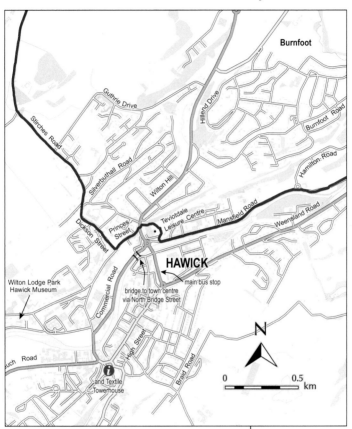

To follow the Borders Abbeys Way and avoid the town centre, turn right to go uphill on the Teviotdale Leisure Centre access road, just before Mansfield Road meets the large roundabout.

STAGE 5
Hawick to Selkirk

Start	Hawick (NT 505 153; Teviotdale Leisure Centre)
Finish	Selkirk (NT 469 284; Market Place)
Distance	12.6 miles (20.3km)
Ascent	583m
Time	5hr 15min
Maps	Landranger 79 and 80; Explorer 331 and 338
Refreshments	Pubs, shops, takeaways, restaurants and cafés in Selkirk
Public transport	Buses link Hawick with: Newtown St Boswells, Denholm, Jedburgh, Melrose, Selkirk, Edinburgh, Kelso, Galashiels Transport Interchange and Berwick-upon-Tweed

Leaving Hawick, the Way ascends steeply out of the town on a minor road before levelling to more gently undulating terrain grazed by livestock, with impressive views to the east. The route then skirts the edge of Drinkstone Hill and passes through a relatively large conifer plantation (Ashkirk Forest) and Woll Golf Course, before joining a minor road and ascending to Bishop's Stone (337m), the highest point on the Borders Abbeys Way, and through a landscape of rushes, sedges and moor grass redolent of the Southern Uplands further west. The route then descends through Hartwoodmyres Forest and traverses farmland before entering The Haining, a neglected country estate on the edge of Selkirk. This stage ends at Market Place in the village centre. Selkirk has a remote feel and is a gateway to the bleak but enchanting Southern Uplands, accessed by the Ettrick and Yarrow valleys to the west.

Continue past Teviotdale Leisure Centre and bear left along an asphalt path through a small park. Cross the A7 and turn left, heading downhill for a few metres before turning right onto Princes Street. Continue along Princes Street for 200 metres and then turn right onto Dickson Street, heading uphill. Dickson Street becomes Stirches Road. This is a fairly steep section that ascends out of the town northwards for about 1.5 miles (2.4km) before levelling out between drystone walls with grand views to the east.

About 680 metres after passing through a minor crossroads, the asphalt ends, and the Way becomes an unsurfaced farm track. The track forks a few metres uphill of **Tandlaw Farm**. Take the left fork, passing through a metal gate. This stone-paved section is a former drove road.

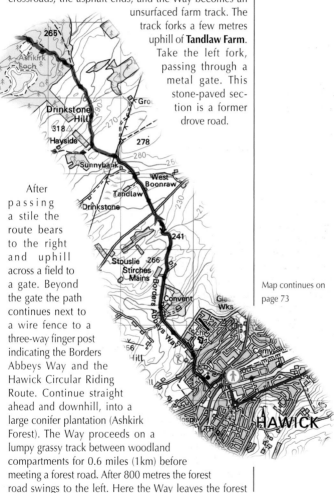

Map continues on page 73

After passing a stile the route bears to the right and uphill across a field to a gate. Beyond the gate the path continues next to a wire fence to a three-way finger post indicating the Borders Abbeys Way and the Hawick Circular Riding Route. Continue straight ahead and downhill, into a large conifer plantation (Ashkirk Forest). The Way proceeds on a lumpy grassy track between woodland compartments for 0.6 miles (1km) before meeting a forest road. After 800 metres the forest road swings to the left. Here the Way leaves the forest

The winding road out of Hawick

Beware airborne golf balls when traversing Woll Golf Course.

road and continues straight ahead on a dirt track, wending downhill to join another forest road.

Continue straight on between a house (**Salenside**) and a shed. A few metres downhill the track crosses the Ale Water via a footbridge and joins a minor asphalt road, where you turn right. A few metres down the road turn left and go over a stile to follow a field edge to another stile and bear left onto **Woll Golf Course**. ◀

Following the waymarkers, cross Woll Burn in the middle of the golf course via the wooden footbridge. The path doubles back to the right on the other side of the burn. Angling left shortly after the bridge, the Way crosses a fairway to the west side of a small broadleaf woodland strip. On reaching the woodland bear left. The Way then skirts a green, heads uphill and continues for 800 metres through the golf course adjacent to a long drystone wall. Continue past a BAW waymarker next to the tenth tee.

The section of path in the vicinity of Woll Golf Course is known locally as **Thief's Road**, named after the notorious Moss Troopers who would regularly use this route. Moss Troopers, much like the earlier Borders Reivers, were lawless brigands who preyed on civilians.

The path then angles up a grassy bank and enters a conifer woodland (Blaeberry Plantation), still adjacent to the drystone wall. Passing through several stiles, the Way levels off, and **Wollrig House** is just visible to the right. The path then doglegs right then left to emerge onto a minor asphalt road. Turn left onto the road.

Continue north-west along the road for 1.3 miles (2.1km), passing the Bishop's Stone (obscured by vegetation on the left of the road), then turn right at a waypost into Hartwoodmyres Forest.

Map continues on page 74

The **Bishop's Stone** is built into the base of the wall, but probably stood on its own in the past. Its name suggests that it may have marked a boundary of the territory belonging to the Bishop of Glasgow, whose extensive estate included virtually all the land of Ashkirk parish at the beginning of the 12th century.

The Way continues along a graded forest road between conifer compartments. **Bowhill House** is visible downhill to the left.

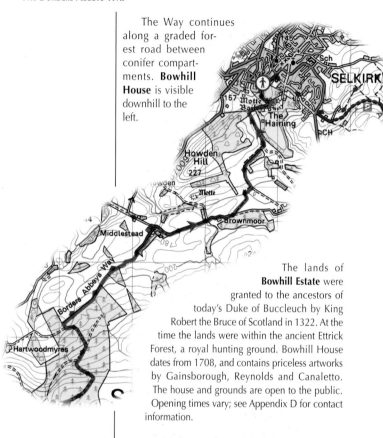

The lands of **Bowhill Estate** were granted to the ancestors of today's Duke of Buccleuch by King Robert the Bruce of Scotland in 1322. At the time the lands were within the ancient Ettrick Forest, a royal hunting ground. Bowhill House dates from 1708, and contains priceless artworks by Gainsborough, Reynolds and Canaletto. The house and grounds are open to the public. Opening times vary; see Appendix D for contact information.

The Way starts heading downhill on the forest road, which wends left and right. It then leaves the forest road at a bend and continues on a grassy track between woodland compartments.

A bench with a view down to Bowhill Estate makes for a pleasant spot to enjoy the scenery.

After 75 metres the track turns to the right and continues next to a wire fence for about 520 metres to a stile, with fields and good views on your left and woodland to your right. ◀

Cross a wire fence via the stile and continue downhill on a farm access track with fields on both sides. The path then joins a larger track, passing through the yard of **Middlestead Farm**. Just beyond the farmyard turn right onto a minor asphalt road.

Continue on the road for 0.7 miles (1.1km), passing **Brownmoor Farm**, and then turn left, going over a stile into a field. The Way continues along the field's edge. At the bottom of the field, cross two stiles and a wooden footbridge into another field. Turn right and continue for 127 metres traversing two more fields. At the corner of the second field turn left onto a grassy track and continue for 700 metres through a series of fields to a waymarker next to a galvanised gate.

Turn left at the waymarker onto a track traversing a field. Haining Loch is occasionally visible beyond some trees to your right. Just past the remains of a dovecot, cross a stile and pass an interpretation panel which displays walking routes and information on **The Haining** estate. The path heads downhill and joins the dilapidated asphalt drive of The Haining mansion, passing in front of the building.

The faded grandeur of The Haining

SELKIRK

Selkirk is an ancient Royal Burgh whose name is derived from the Old English *sele cirici* (Church (or Kirk) in the Forest). William Wallace was apparently proclaimed Guardian of Scotland within the town's kirk in 1298. *Sele* is probably a reference to the ancient Forest of Ettrick. The Celtic tribe that once lived in this forest were known to the Romans as the *Selgovae*, meaning hunters of the forest. The forest was a royal hunting reserve in medieval times but it has since disappeared due to timber harvesting and sheep grazing.

The famous explorer Mungo Park was born at Foulshiels near Selkirk in 1771, and was an apprentice surgeon in Selkirk. He was friends with Sir Walter Scott, and used to meet him at the Forest Club, a gentlemen's club that convened in the County Hotel in Selkirk's town centre. Park died on the Niger River in West Africa after a skirmish with natives in 1806.

Sir Walter Scott served as Sheriff of Selkirk for 33 years. Sir Walter Scott's Courtroom Museum, located just behind his statue in Market Place (Apr–Sept Mon–Fri 10am–4pm, Sat 11am–3pm; May–Aug also Sun 11am–3pm; Oct Mon–Sat 12–3pm; closed during June's Selkirk Common Riding) features an audiovisual presentation of his association with the town, while Halliwell's House Museum (late Mar–Oct Mon–Sat 11am–4pm, Sun 12–3pm), also located in Market Place, offers an insight into historic Selkirk.

The Haining estate was originally owned by the Pringle family, whose ancestors were a powerful reiving group. The mansion, built next to the remains of the medieval Selkirk Castle, dates back to the 1790s and has been heavily modified internally, particularly during World War II, when it was used as an army base. The house is usually closed to the public.

Follow the asphalt drive downhill, passing under the entrance archway onto West Port, a suburban street. Cross the street and turn right, heading uphill to Market Place, Selkirk's town centre.

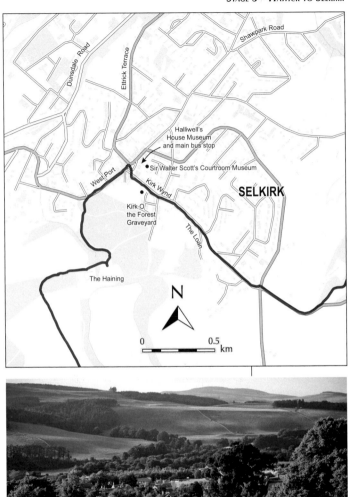

Selkirk is the gateway to the remote Ettrick and Yarrow valleys

STAGE 6
Selkirk to Tweedbank

Start	Selkirk (NT 469 284; Market Place)
Finish	Near Tweedbank railway station (NT 529 347)
Distance	8.9 miles (14.4km)
Ascent	336m
Time	3hr 35min
Maps	Landranger 73; Explorer 338
Refreshments	Café at Abbotsford House, snack outlet at Tweedbank railway station
Public transport	Buses link Selkirk with: Newtown St Boswells, Hawick, Melrose, Edinburgh, Galashiels Transport Interchange and Carlisle

This beginning of this stage of the route provides some striking views to the north. The Way ascends gently from Selkirk town to Selkirk Hill, a haven for a variety of birds and plants, then continues through farmland, making use of an old drove road, before descending at a gentle gradient to skirt Cauldshiels Loch and pass Abbotsford House, the grand former residence of Sir Walter Scott. If time allows, a visit to the house and grounds is recommended. The house contains a unique array of Scottish artefacts collected by Scott. The Way then follows the banks of the Tweed downriver to Tweedbank. This final stage of the Way finishes 600 metres from Tweedbank railway terminus.

Within the graveyard you can view the grave of the maternal ancestors of former American president Franklin D Roosevelt.

From Market Place head uphill on Kirk Wynd, passing the ruins of the Kirk o' the Forest and its graveyard. ◄

Continue uphill at the crossroads, where Kirk Wynd becomes The Loan, changing to South Port, before carefully crossing the A7, and continue along the pavement of the road opposite (A699) for 285 metres before bearing left onto a footpath skirting **Selkirk Golf Course**. Be careful when crossing the A7.

This is **Selkirk Hill**, a haven for birds and plants. Here the path traverses an interesting landscape of

The Kirk o' the Forest graveyard

gorse bushes and open grassy areas. The views to the north on a clear day are impressive.

After 520 metres bear left at a fork in the path, passing a shelter with a red roof. About 320 metres after the shelter, the Way joins another track. Bear left at this junction, and after 95 metres, pass through a wooden gate onto a vehicle track in front of a house. Turn right and continue along the track for 0.6 miles (1km) before going through a gate into a field. A bench in the field provides a comfortable spot to enjoy the views.

Cross the field, angling uphill and heading north. At the other side of the field, go through a gate into an adjacent field. The path follows a hedge on your left-hand side. Continue through a couple of gates to join a minor asphalt road.

Keep going on the road for 0.9 miles (1.5km) before turning left opposite a large radio mast onto an unsurfaced vehicle track via a gate. Follow the track downhill past a house (**Woodlands**) and outbuildings, cross a minor asphalt road, and continue on the track, which was once a drove road.

Plaque at the Kirk o' the Forest graveyard

Follow the undulating track adjacent to a drystone wall for 1.8 miles (2.9km), through a series of gates and fields. This area has a relatively remote feel to it.

The Way continues on a beech-flanked track, also bounded by drystone walls, and descends towards **Cauldshiels Loch**.

Keep an eye out for an easily missed waymarker indicating right to Cauldshiels Loch. If you reach a minor asphalt road, you've missed the waymarker and gone too far!

Turn right at the waymarker next to a wooden gate to enter a small broadleaf woodland and skirt the northern edge of the loch, before turning sharply to the left. The Way then leaves the woodland to join a minor unsurfaced access road. When the track joins a minor asphalt road, turn right.

Map continues on page 82

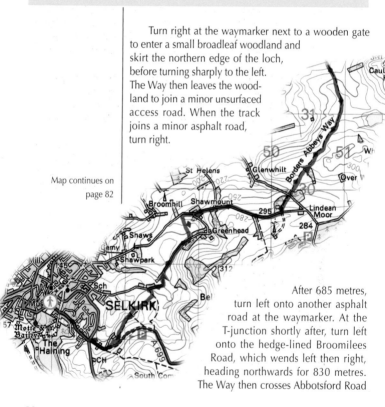

After 685 metres, turn left onto another asphalt road at the waymarker. At the T-junction shortly after, turn left onto the hedge-lined Broomilees Road, which wends left then right, heading northwards for 830 metres. The Way then crosses Abbotsford Road

(B6360) to pass in front of **Abbotsford House**, the impressive former residence of Sir Walter Scott.

Passing Abbotsford House, continue downhill on a track towards the River Tweed, following a waymarker pointing to Melrose. A few metres from the Tweed a waymarker indicates the Way to the right. However, if you bear left at the track opposite this waymarker you can follow the Tweed upriver for a few hundred metres to get

ABBOTSFORD HOUSE

Built in 1824, Abbotsford House is named after a former nearby ford where abbots would cross the Tweed going to and from Melrose Abbey. Scott was a prolific collector and used Abbotsford to display his eclectic array of antique curiosities, armaments, furniture and books. However, Abbotsford cost a fortune to build, and Scott had to write prolifically to create the necessary income.

The house, set in a garden designed by Scott, and the accompanying visitor centre, are managed by the National Trust for Scotland. The visitor centre (Mar 10am–4pm; Apr–Oct 10am–5pm; Nov 10am–4pm) includes a gift shop, restaurant, displays and public toilets. An entry ticket allows multiple visits for up to one year.

Abbotsford House (photo supplied by The Abbotsford Trust)

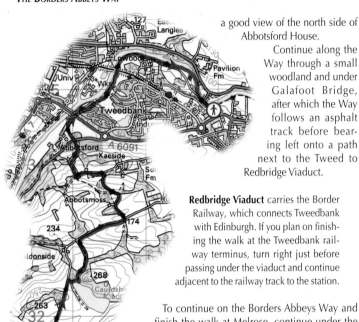

a good view of the north side of Abbotsford House.

Continue along the Way through a small woodland and under Galafoot Bridge, after which the Way follows an asphalt track before bearing left onto a path next to the Tweed to Redbridge Viaduct.

Redbridge Viaduct carries the Border Railway, which connects Tweedbank with Edinburgh. If you plan on finishing the walk at the Tweedbank railway terminus, turn right just before passing under the viaduct and continue adjacent to the railway track to the station.

To continue on the Borders Abbeys Way and finish the walk at Melrose, continue under the viaduct. The path remains adjacent to the Tweed for 0.9 miles (1.5km) before joining the asphalt driveway of **Lowood House**. Turn left into the driveway, passing the dilapidated former entrance lodge, to meet the busy B6374. ◀

Cross the B6374 with caution.

Turn right on the pavement on the opposite side of the **B6374** and continue uphill for 115 metres to the wooden gate and waymarker indicating the path to Melrose via the wooden gate described in Stage 1.

APPENDIX A

Facilities available on each Stage of the Borders Abbeys Way

Stage	Place	B&B / hotel	Campsite	Restaurant	Pub / café	Take-away	Shop
1	Melrose	✓ (1)	✓	✓	✓	✓	✓
1	Newtown St Boswells	✓ (3)			✓	✓	✓
1 (alt)	St Boswells	✓ (3)		✓	✓	✓	✓
2	Dryburgh	✓ (3)					
2	Clintmains	✓ (3)					
2	Kelso	✓ (1)		✓	✓	✓	✓
3	Jedburgh	✓ (1)	✓	✓	✓	✓	✓
4	Denholm	✓ (2)		✓	✓		✓
4	Hornshole		✓				
4	Hawick	✓ (1)		✓	✓	✓	✓
5	Selkirk	✓ (2)		✓	✓	✓	✓
6	Abbotsford House				✓ Café		

Note: In the B&B/hotel column, 1 represents a wide choice; 3 represents a limited choice, with perhaps only one establishment available. This table does not reflect accommodation available on the Airbnb or Booking.com websites.

APPENDIX B

Accommodation

Melrose

The Townhouse Hotel
tel 01896 822645
www.thetownhousemelrose.co.uk

Burts Hotel
tel 01896 822285
www.burtshotel.co.uk

Station Hotel
tel 01896 823 147
www.stationhotelmelrose.com

George & Abbotsford Hotel
tel 01896 822 308
enquiries@georgeandabbotsford.co.uk

Old Bank House B&B
tel 01896 823712

Dunfermline House B&B
tel 01896 822411
www.dunfermlinehouse.co.uk

Braidwood B&B
tel 01896 822488
www.braidwoodmelrose.co.uk

Fiorlin B&B
tel 01896 822984
www.melrosebedandbreakfast.co.uk

Newtown St Boswells

Dryburgh Arms Hotel
tel 01835 822704
www.dryburgharms.co.uk

St Boswells

Buccleuch Arms Hotel
tel 01835 822243
www.buccleucharms.com

Sunnyknowe B&B
tel 01835 824319
www.sunnyknowebandb.com

Dryburgh Abbey Hotel
tel 01896 822651
www.dryburgh.co.uk

Clint Lodge
tel 01835 822027
www.clintlodge.co.uk

Kelso

Ednam House Hotel
tel 01573 224168
www.ednamhouse.com

Queens Head Hotel
tel 01573 228899
www.queensheadhotelkelso.com

Cross Keys Hotel
tel 01573 223303
www.cross-keys-hotel.co.uk

The Black Swan Hotel
tel 01573 224563
www.theblackswanhotel.co.uk

Inglestone House (guesthouse)
tel 01573 225800
www.inglestonehouse.com

The Townhouse B&B
tel 07711 157060
www.thetownhousekelso.co.uk

Abbeyside B&B
tel 01573 223915

The Central Guesthouse
(self-catering only)
tel 07419 826000
www.thecentralguesthousekelso.co.uk

Jedburgh
Glenbank House Hotel
tel 01835 862 258
www.jedburgh-hotel.com

The Capon Tree Town House
tel 01835 869596
www.thecapontree.com

Maedhon Guest House
tel 01835 862504
www.meadhon.co.uk

Willow Court B&B
tel 01835 863702

Glenfriars House B&B
tel 01835 862492
www.glenfriars.com

Airenlea B&B
tel 01835 862216
www.airenlea.co.uk

Denholm
The Auld Cross Keys Inn
tel 01450 870305
www.crosskeysdenholm.co.uk

Fox and Hounds Inn
tel 01450 870247

Hawick
Elm House Hotel
tel 01450 372866 / 374175

Mansfield House Hotel
tel 01450 360400
www.themansfieldhousehotel.com

Brougham House B&B
tel 07814 354106

Bridge House Guest House
tel 01450 370701
www.hawickhotel.co.uk

The Bank Guesthouse
tel 01450 363760 / 07595 256715
www.thebankno12highst.com

Selkirk
County Hotel
tel 01750 721233
www.countyhotelselkirk.co.uk

The Glen Hotel
tel 01750 20259
www.glenhotel.co.uk

Tower Street Guesthouse
tel 01750 21481 / 07745 898787
www.towerstreetselkirk.com

Ivy Bank B&B
tel 01750 21270

Note: While no accommodation is available in Tweedbank itself, accommodation is available in Galashiels (approximately 2 miles/3.2km from Tweedbank) and Melrose.

APPENDIX C
Public transport information

For train tickets and information
www.nationalrail.co.uk
www.scotrail.co.uk
www.thetrainline.com

For bus tickets and information
www.traveline.info

Borders Buses
tel 01289 308719 / 01896 754350
www.bordersbuses.co.uk

Telford's Coaches
tel 01387 375677
www.telfordscoaches.com

Scottish Borders Council bus services
tel 0300 1001 800
www.scotborders.gov.uk

Peter Hogg
tel 01835 863755
www.roadhoggs.net

BUS SERVICE INFORMATION

Stage 1: Tweedbank to Newtown St Boswells

Buses to and from Tweedbank railway station

Bus Number	Destination	Operator
61	*Galashiels Transport Interchange	Borders Buses
67	**Melrose, Newtown St Boswells, St Boswells	Borders Buses
72	Selkirk, Melrose	Borders Buses
964	Galashiels Transport Interchange, Newtown St Boswells	Scottish Borders Council
X62	Melrose, Edinburgh	Borders Buses

*Weekends only.
**Weekends only, and only on the Galashiels to St Boswells service. The 67 service going to and from Berwick-upon-Tweed does not stop at Tweedbank railway station. Trains to and from Edinburgh approximately every half hour from Tweedbank railway station (free parking) and Galashiels Transport Interchange.

Buses to and from Melrose

Bus Number	Destination	Operator
60	Galashiels Transport Interchange, Berwick-upon-Tweed	Borders Buses
61	*Galashiels Transport Interchange	Borders Buses
67	Berwick-upon-Tweed**, Tweedbank railway station***, Galashiels Transport Interchange, St Boswells, Kelso	Borders Buses
68	Jedburgh, Galashiels Transport Interchange	Borders Buses
71	Galashiels Transport Interchange	Borders Buses
72	Selkirk, Tweedbank railway station	Borders Buses
504	Hawick, Selkirk, Kelso, St Boswells, Galashiels Transport Interchange	Telford's Coaches
964	Galashiels Transport Interchange, Tweedbank railway station, Newtown St Boswells	Scottish Borders Council
X62	Edinburgh, Tweedbank railway station	Borders Buses
X95	Edinburgh, Hawick, Selkirk, Galashiels Transport Interchange, Carlisle	Borders Buses

*Weekends only.
**Buses to and from Berwick-upon-Tweed stop at Berwick railway station.
***Weekends only, and only on the Galashiels to St Boswells service.
Service 67 stops at Clintmains road end; useful if you only want to walk half of Stage 2.
X95 stops at the Borders General Hospital, on the south side of the A6091, just outside Melrose.

Stage 2: Newtown St Boswells to Kelso

Buses to and from Newtown St Boswells

Bus Number	Destination	Operator
51	Jedburgh, St Boswells, Edinburgh	Borders Buses
52	Kelso, St Boswells, Edinburgh	Borders Buses
67	Berwick-upon-Tweed*, Kelso, St Boswells, Galashiels Transport Interchange, Melrose	Borders Buses
68	Jedburgh, Galashiels Transport Interchange, St Boswells, Melrose	Borders Buses
964	Tweedbank railway station, Melrose, Galashiels Transport Interchange	Scottish Borders Council

*Buses to and from Berwick-upon-Tweed stop at Berwick railway station.
Local timetables only state Newtown (missing out 'St Boswells'). The Royal Bank bus stop refers to a branch of the Royal Bank of Scotland, which is now closed.
Service 67 stops at Clintmains road end; useful if you only want to walk half of Stage 2.

Stage 3: Kelso to Jedburgh

Buses to and from Kelso

Bus Number	Destination	Operator
20	Hawick, Denholm, Jedburgh*	Peter Hogg, Borders Buses
52	St Boswells, Edinburgh	Borders Buses
67	Berwick-upon-Tweed**, Newtown St Boswells, St Boswells, Galashiels Transport Interchange, Melrose	Borders Buses
131	Newcastle upon Tyne main coach station	Peter Hogg
504	Hawick, Selkirk, Melrose, Newtown St Boswells	Telford's Coaches
710	Newcastle upon Tyne (Metrocentre)	Glen Valley Travel

*Peter Hogg operates Service 20 from Monday to Saturday and Borders Buses operates the service on Sundays.
**Buses to and from Berwick-upon-Tweed stop at Berwick railway station.
Service 67 stops at Clintmains road end – useful if you only want to walk half of Stage 2.

Stage 4: Jedburgh to Hawick

Buses to and from Jedburgh

Bus Number	Destination	Operator
20	Kelso, Denholm, Hawick*	Peter Hogg and Borders Buses
51	St Boswells, Newtown St Boswells, Edinburgh	Borders Buses
68	St Boswells, Newtown St Boswells, Melrose, Galashiels Transport Interchange	Borders Buses
131	Newcastle upon Tyne main coach station	Peter Hogg

*Peter Hogg operates Service 20 from Monday to Saturday and Borders Buses operates the service on Sundays.

Stage 5: Hawick to Selkirk

Buses to and from Hawick

Bus Number	Destination	Operator
20	Kelso, Denholm, Jedburgh*	Peter Hogg and Borders Buses
503	Berwick-upon-Tweed**	Telford's Coaches
504	Selkirk, Newtown St Boswells, Melrose	Telford's Coaches
X95	Edinburgh, Selkirk, Melrose***, Galashiels Transport Interchange, Carlisle	Borders Buses

*Peter Hogg operates Service 20 from Monday to Saturday and Borders Buses operates the service on Sundays.
**Service 503 from Hawick to Berwick-upon-Tweed stops at Berwick railway station. Buses going in the opposite direction (from Berwick-upon-Tweed to Hawick) depart from Golden Square in Berwick town centre.
***X95 stops at Borders General Hospital, on the south side of the A6091, just outside Melrose.

Stage 6: Selkirk to Tweedbank

Buses to and from Selkirk

Bus Number	Destination	Operator
73	Galashiels Transport Interchange	Borders Buses
504	Hawick, Newtown St Boswells, Melrose	Telford's Coaches
X95	Edinburgh, Hawick, Melrose*, Galashiels Transport Interchange, Carlisle	Borders Buses

*X95 stops at Borders General Hospital, on the south side of the A6091, just outside Melrose.

APPENDIX D
Useful contacts

Tourist information centres
www.visitscotland.com

Jedburgh
Murray's Green
tel 01835 863 170

Hawick
1 Tower Mill
Heart of Hawick
tel 01450 373993

Walking Support
Luggage transfer service
tel 01896 822079
www.walkingsupport.co.uk

Historic Environment Scotland (HES)
Explorer Passes for Borders abbeys
and historic houses
tel 0131 668 8999
www.historicenvironment.scot

Scottish Natural Heritage (SNH)
Outdoor Access Code and information
on enjoying Scotland's natural
environment
www.nature.scot/
scottish-outdoor-access-code

Scottish Borders Council (SBC)
Countryside Ranger Service
tel 01835 826750
www.scotborders.gov.uk

**Trimontium Trust and Three Hills
Roman Heritage Centre**
Melrose
tel 01896 822651
www.trimontium.org.uk

Bowhill House and Estate
Selkirk
tel 01750 22204
www.bowhillhouse.co.uk

Airbnb
Online booking service for homestays
and private accommodation
www.airbnb.com

Booking.com
Online booking service for hotels
and B&Bs
www.booking.com

**For sick, injured or distressed animals
or birds**
RSPCA
tel 0300 1234 999
www.rspca.org.uk

APPENDIX E
Further reading

Borders reivers

Durham, Keith. *Strongholds of the Border Reivers: Fortifications of the Anglo-Scottish Border 1296–1603* (Osprey Publishing Ltd, 2008). This book examines Border fortresses, ranging from small, well-defended castles to imposing tower houses, or 'peles', and a variety of fortified farmhouses known as 'bastles'.

Moffat, Alistair. *The Reivers: The Story of the Border Reivers* (Birlinn Ltd, 2017) The story of the Reivers and their lives on the frontier is brought to life in this book.

Ordnance Survey. *In Search of the Border Reivers: An Historical Map and Guide* (Produced in conjunction with the Royal Commissions on Historical Monuments for England, Scotland and Wales, 1998).

History of the Borders landscape

Cruft, Kitty; Dunbar, John; Fawcett, Richard. *Borders: Buildings of Scotland* (Pevsner Architectural Guides: Buildings of Scotland) (Yale University Press, 2006). A thorough guide to historical architecture in the Scottish Borders.

Moffat, Alistair. *The Borders* (Birlinn Ltd, 2007). A comprehensive book describing the history of the landscape and people of the Borders, from the first colonisation of the Wildwood to the present.

Rackham, Oliver. *History of the Countryside* (Phoenix Press, 2000). Using old maps, place-names, archaeological remains and other historical sources, Rackham explains how the countryside has been used by man over the centuries. Although the book explores the British landscape, it is still relevant to the Borders.

Whittemore, Colin. *Farming Stories from the Scottish Borders: Hard Lives for Poor Reward* (Old Pond Publishing Ltd, 2017). The landscape we see today appears bucolic, but the lives of people who worked the land for wealthy estate owners were often hard. Whittemore tells the story of rural life in the Borders over a 300-year period in this collection of intimate accounts.

Medieval Scotland

MacQuarie, Alan. *Medieval Scotland: Kingship and Nation* (The History Press, 2004). MacQuarie's book provides a solid background to Medieval Scotland and will enhance a visit to the Borders abbeys.

Morris, Marc. *A Great and Terrible King: Edward I and the Forging of Britain* (Windmill Books, 2009). Edward I was King of England from 1272 to 1307 and was known as 'The Hammer of Scotland' due to his brutal oppression of the Scots during his reign. Morris's biography provides a thorough account of this formidable king.

Oram, Richard. *David I: The King Who Made Scotland* (The History Press, 2008). An in-depth study of the king who brought Norman Monasticism to Scotland and founded the Borders abbeys.

DOWNLOAD THE ROUTES
IN GPX FORMAT

All the routes in this guide are available for download from:

www.cicerone.co.uk/980/GPX

as GPX files. You should be able to load them into most formats of mobile device, whether GPS or smartphone.

When you go to this link, you will be asked for your email address and where you purchased the guide, and have the option to subscribe to the Cicerone e-newsletter.

www.cicerone.co.uk

IF YOU ENJOYED THIS GUIDEBOOK YOU MIGHT ALSO BE INTERESTED IN...

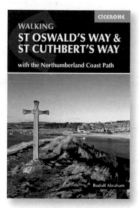

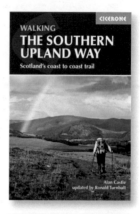

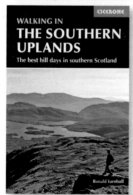

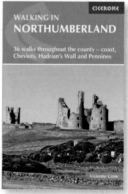

SELECTION OF UK CICERONE GUIDES

For full information on all our guides,
books and eBooks, visit our website:
www.cicerone.co.uk

Walking – Trekking – Mountaineering – Climbing – Cycling

Over 40 years, Cicerone have built up an outstanding collection of over 300 guides, inspiring all sorts of amazing adventures.

 Every guide comes from extensive exploration and research by our expert authors, all with a passion for their subjects. They are frequently praised, endorsed and used by clubs, instructors and outdoor organisations.

All our titles can now be bought as **e-books**, **ePubs** and **Kindle** files and we also have an online magazine – **Cicerone Extra** – with features to help cyclists, climbers, walkers and trekkers choose their next adventure, at home or abroad.

Our website shows any **new information** we've had in since a book was published. Please do let us know if you find anything has changed, so that we can publish the latest details. On our **website** you'll also find great ideas and lots of detailed information about what's inside every guide and you can buy **individual routes** from many of them online.

It's easy to keep in touch with what's going on at Cicerone by getting our monthly **free e-newsletter**, which is full of offers, competitions, up-to-date information and topical articles. You can subscribe on our home page and also follow us on **Facebook** and **Twitter** or dip into our **blog**.

Cicerone – the very best guides for exploring the world.

CICERONE

Juniper House, Murley Moss, Oxenholme Road, Kendal, Cumbria LA9 7RL
Tel: 015395 62069 info@cicerone.co.uk
www.cicerone.co.uk